PERCY THROWER

My Lifetime of Gardening

Best Wishes
Percy Thrower

HAMLYN
London · New York · Sydney · Toronto

PERCY THROWER

My Lifetime of Gardening

Percy Thrower with Ronald Webber

Contents

Gardener's Lad   6

Royal Bothy Days   31

Life in the Parks   56

The Town of Flowers   73

Britain's Head Gardener   88

The Magnolias   106

Man of Business   127

Favourites of a Lifetime   140

Pleasures and Rewards   160

Acknowledgements   176

First published in 1977 by
The Hamlyn Publishing Group Limited
LONDON · NEW YORK · SYDNEY · TORONTO
Astronaut House, Feltham, Middlesex, England

Copyright © The Hamlyn Publishing Group, 1977
ISBN 0 600 35519 5

Printed in Hong Kong by
Leefung-Asco Printers Limited

Filmset in England by
Tradespools Limited, Frome, Somerset
Set in 12 on 14 pt Monophoto Apollo

Gardener's lad

Here, in the peace of my garden at The Magnolias, looking out over the glorious panorama of the Shropshire countryside, there are times when I think back to the changes which I, and people like me, have seen in a long working lifetime.

For the changes have been almost unbelievable. Neither our grandparents nor our parents experienced anything like them. For, up until, say, the turn of the century life went on more or less as it had for generations past. Today television brings happenings the world over almost instantly into our sitting rooms while air travel has turned old attitudes about distance upside down. It is hardly to be wondered at that the kind of life I lived when young now seems a far-away dream.

I was born, the second son of a family of three boys and two girls, in a cottage on a large Buckinghamshire estate on January 30th, 1913 – the estate where my father was head gardener and where I was to grow up with but one ambition and that was to become a head gardener like him.

The estate belonged to the Denny family and it was in the early years of this century that Frederick Denny, an Irish bacon millionaire, built a new mansion, Horwood House, on the site of a former rectory house and then looked round for somebody to remake and look after the gardens. My father became that man, and whatever I may have achieved in life must in large part be due to that decision, for it was there, as a fourteen-year-old boy, that I began my professional gardening career and acquired the grounding which allowed me to go on to other things.

Both my parents came from East Anglia: Father from Felixstowe and Mother from Walberswick. Early in life Father decided to become a gardener and after a period

Percy John Thrower, aged six months, with Mother, Father and brother Harry

of training at Bawdsey Manor near Woodbridge (owned by Sir Cuthbert Quilter) he moved to King's Waldenbury near Hitchin in Hertfordshire as a journeyman-gardener, later becoming foreman. It was while he was at King's Waldenbury that he received the offer from the Dennys (Mrs Denny was a Quilter of Bawdsey Manor and knew my father) to go to Horwood House as head gardener.

Horwood was my home for the first eighteen years of my life so naturally the memory of it stays unforgettably with me.

The house itself, I have been told, is a copy of a William and Mary house that Frederick Denny had seen somewhere in the West Country. It was built by Cubitts under the direction of the architect Detmar Blow. Though it was still quite new when first I made its acquaintance it always seemed to have a soft, mellow, long-established

7

look, probably because of the special russety bricks imported from Holland and the genuine old tiles used for the gabled roof. The windows, too, were leaded to help with the old-world effect. An entrance porch with stone seats and a massive oak door led into a hall with stone floor, oak panelling and an open fireplace above which was the coat-of-arms of the Denny family. Leading out from here was a drawing room, dining room and library which by pulling back dividing sets of double doors could be turned into a fine reception suite for entertaining. Upstairs were what was known as the boudoir together with fourteen bed and dressing rooms and five bathrooms. Separate from the house proper in a west wing were the staff quarters with nine bedrooms.

Grouped around the house yard were various outbuildings including a butler's room, drying room, boot,

Horwood House, Buckinghamshire, the home of the Denny family. The author's father was head gardener here for much of his life.

knife and bicycle rooms, as well as stores for coal and wood. The garage took four cars and had three rooms attached for chauffeurs. The thatched stables were in a quadrangle with a house for the head groom built in, as well as rooms for the stable boys. Separate from all this was the six-roomed head gardener's cottage in which I was born.

The estate proper had two farms, eleven cottages, parkland, plantations and, of course, the gardens: in all it covered four hundred and eighty-two acres. The small village of Little Horwood more or less joined on to the estate; the nearest railway station was Swanbourne half a mile away on the Bletchley, Banbury and Oxford branch line. The nearest town was Winslow which was two and a half miles away; Bletchley was six miles, Buckingham seven and a half, Aylesbury twelve and London (reached by express train from Bletchley) fifty-one miles. When my father first took over what later became the gardens it was bare fields and woodland. But by the time I was old enough to appreciate horticultural matters the gardens were well established. A

The drawing room of Horwood House

ha-ha (the first I ever saw) gave an unbroken view across the parklands where horses and cattle grazed. Large lawns abounded and many had been allowed to retain old trees – chestnuts, cedars, oaks, elms and ashes – to give them that mature look that such trees can confer. A lime avenue over a quarter of a mile long ran from the forecourt of the house to the lodge gates and I can remember being told that when the trees were being planted the gardeners found thousands of broken beer bottles left behind by the workmen who had built the drive. Overlooked from the drawing-room of the house was what was known as an étang – it is a word not often met with these days – a rectangular pond, in this case surrounded by yew trees, rose borders and paths of flagstones, a rock-garden covering nearly an acre and a half, a herbaceous border and more lawns sweeping away.

The kitchen garden of about two acres was enclosed by walls ten feet high and held the greenhouses – a lean-to, carnation house, propagating house and one in which melons and cucumbers were grown – all of which, erected by an old Bristol firm, Skinner Board, were constructed of metal, with metal clips to hold in the glass. Though good houses in most ways, they had an unfortunate tendency to drip condensation everywhere. They were heated by hot water with anthracite as fuel. Near the greenhouses was the potting shed which also served as my father's office. The south borders in the kitchen garden grew early potatoes (May Queen, Sharpe's Express, Midlothian Early), early lettuce and early French beans; the north borders held the later crops of this type. The maincrop vegetables were in four plots, each plot edged with box which was always a nuisance, for though it looked attractive it harboured slugs and snails as well as requiring an undue amount of attention – especially clipping. From the centre of the garden wide steps led down to broad herbaceous borders on either side, each with a background of old rambling roses like American Pillar, Minnehaha, Hiawatha, Dorothy Perkins, Caroline Testout and Emily Gray. The centre itself had a round pond with fountain and lead cherubim and was planted with water-lilies; and *Cotoneaster horizontalis* had been arranged so as to cover the inlet of the water supply. The

The head gardener's cottage, set among trees at the end of the orchard

south-facing wall had fan-trained peaches and nectarines; the east sweet cherries; the north Morello cherry, apples and pears; and the west more apples and pears but on this side grown as espaliers.

All this was to become even more familiar to me when, at the age of fourteen, I started to work full time for my father.

While still at school I had already been in the habit of helping Father on Saturday mornings and summer evenings. And he had given me a small garden of my own under a walnut tree at the back of our cottage. This was not, looking back, the best place for a garden, for it was shady and the roots of the tree made the soil difficult to cultivate besides taking most of the goodness out of the ground. But I doubt if I worried about that in those days. I also had my own garden at school. I went to the Church of England school in the village where my teachers were Mr and Mrs Davies and the number of children attending was rarely above forty. I have to admit I was never particularly bright at school; except at gardening. I did enjoy that. With Father a head gardener I was expected to know more about it than the others and my plot had to be an example to them. I grew lettuce, radish, carrots, beetroot, beans, peas and a few flowers in the form of hardy annuals. Occasionally I gave the headmaster (who was a keen gardener himself) a hand with his garden. So when I reached the age of fourteen I was only too eager to leave school and go to work with my father.

My youthful age gave me no privileges. My hours were the same as the other gardeners: I started at 6.30 in the morning, had a break of half an hour for breakfast at 8, an hour for dinner from 12.30 until 1.30 and finished at 5.30 (1.30 of a Saturday) and when necessary overtime had to be worked. A long day for a lad of fourteen. Yet Mrs Denny, the lady of the house, maintained that a shilling a day was plenty for a boy of that age, so at the end of each week I took home six shillings, plus an odd shilling or two for overtime.

To begin with, I worked in the greenhouses under one of the local lads who was training to be a gardener, sweeping floors, crocking pots, cleaning out the stokehole, clinkering the fire, making sure there was always plenty of fuel for the boiler, and suchlike basic jobs. Gradually I was given more responsibility – a little pricking out, some potting up, perhaps.

At work we wore a gardener's apron tied round the waist with a pocket in it for knife, raffia and the various odds and ends that a gardener needs. We had strong substantial boots (Wellingtons had not yet arrived on the scene): if we were so foolhardy as to turn up for work in a pair of shoes we would as like as not be greeted with some sarcastic remark such as 'What've you got your bedroom slippers on for?'

At times I worked with my father. He wasn't the easiest of men to work with. If one of the staff did something that met with his disapproval he was liable to take off his cap and throw it at the offender. I remember it once happening to me. We were getting a batch of statice and calceolarias ready for the Chelsea Flower Show. I was fastening the blooms of the calceolarias with short lengths of wire so that they wouldn't get broken on the journey to London. But I did accidentally break one and before I had even said anything his cap came flying across the greenhouse, hitting me hard. Father was awarded a Banksian medal by the R.H.S. for this exhibit and over the years he won several awards at Chelsea. He also did a good deal of judging locally, including the August Bank Holiday horticultural show at Bletchley and horticultural shows at Wolverton, Whitchurch and other places around.

One must remember that a head gardener of a large estate in those days was almost like the Lord of the Manor. He was looked up to in the locality and feared by most of his staff. They were a clannish lot among themselves: my father's friends included the head gardeners of Mentmore, Luton Hoo, King's Waldenbury and other famous houses and they would discuss things together, pass on information and exchange plants.

Father turned out every morning at 6.30 to see the men start and he was there to see them go midday and evening. And of an evening there was no taking of tools into the toolshed at 5.25 – we took them in at 5.30 and washed, oiled and hung them up in their correct places in *our* time. Every day every tool had to be cared for in this way. The potting shed, too, had to be kept so that one could almost eat one's food off the bench: when we had finished potting for the day we had to heap up the compost that remained and leave it tidy ready for the next morning.

In a typical day Father would go round the gardens to see that the men were carrying out their tasks properly, and at times he would work with the men. When we were making the rock garden, for example, he supervised the positioning of every stone: this was done with crowbars, three or four men round a stone weighing perhaps half a ton, using rounded pieces of wood as rollers. He also liked to do all the pruning of the fruit. No one else was trusted with it except perhaps a foreman and even then Father would stay and watch to see that it was done properly. We young lads certainly weren't allowed to do any pruning – that was an art thought far too high for us!

The author, aged eleven

We would be permitted to watch how it was done, that was all.

Father had his programme of work for the whole year. He would come along and say, 'Time for alpine cuttings,' or 'Better start pruning,' or whatever needed doing at that particular time.

In March he would wait until the dust began to rise from the garden path when he would say: 'Ah! March dust . . . worth a pound a peck'. By which he meant that the surface of the soil was drying and ready for the making of good seedbeds for the vegetables. In April he would often come out with the old saying:

> If the oak be out before the ash
> Then we shall have a splash.
> If the ash be out before the oak
> Then we shall have a thorough soak.

Even today I always look around in April to see how these two trees are faring, but I can't remember ever seeing the ash out before the oak.

Another saying of his was: 'When the gorse is in bloom, love is in season'. Which is an old country joke, for, of course, gorse carries at least a few flowers during the whole twelve months of the year.

We were expected to keep a diary of when we did things and how we did them, including the various composts used. The compost mixing at Horwood House was a major operation. In these days of standardized John Innes and various peat composts it is hard to recall that these have only been with us, more or less, since the last war. Before that a different compost was used for almost every type of plant and each head gardener would have his own favourite compost recipes which he handed on to his staff who dutifully wrote them down and used them in their subsequent careers. At Horwood we took turf from around the rabbit warrens where the grass had been eaten close, stacked the turves with alternate layers of farmyard manure and left the heap for up to a year. This formed the basis of most of our composts and when we started to make one we would chop down the heap with a spade, put the chopped turf into a wheel-barrow and take it into the potting shed where every piece was pulled to bits by hand. Oak and beech leafmould was collected from the woods and the sand had always to be the silver type from Leighton Buzzard. For cyclamen we crushed bricks to give brickdust and also used coal dust. For chrysanthemums we would put quarter-inch bones in the base of each pot instead of crocks: they would still be there when we threw the plants away but the roots would be massed around the bones so it did seem that they must have obtained some nourishment from them. All a very far cry from the ready-mixed and ready-bagged composts of today.

One of the main tasks of the gardening staff was to ensure that flowers were always available for decoration in the House, both flowering plants and cut blooms. And special occasions, of course, demanded special efforts. One of Father's best happened at the golden wedding of the Dennys, after I had left. He erected an arch with golden letters of congratulations to Mr and Mrs Denny written on a red background at the entrance gates to the courtyard on a day when, according to a report in the local paper, 'the beauty of the grounds was enhanced by the sunshine' and over two hundred guests turned up. And there had always to be fresh vegetables and, as far as possible, fresh fruit. This taught me the art of using greenhouses to achieve continuity throughout the twelve months of the year.

A fairly new crop (in those days) for the greenhouse was tomatoes. People were still suspicious of these 'love-apples' as they were often called. In fact, at our house, Mother used to put sugar on them to try and get us youngsters to like them. The variety was Sutton's Best of All, which had ugly fruit something like the later Potentate. Cucumbers were more popular; we grew Improved Telegraph, which is still about today, and we also had plenty of melons, Superlative and King George.

In the kitchen garden deep digging was accepted practice. For both strawberries (Royal Sovereign and a few Tardive de Leopold) and onions we double-trenched, something we never do today. And it was double-trenching, too, for runner beans and seakale. For all this plenty of manure was considered vital, so every morning we wheeled manure from the stables to the garden where it was mixed with compost and left ready for use. Among the more unusual kitchen garden crops were corn salad, chicory, endive, salsify, scorzonera, horseradish (for the making of sauce) and, a rarity today, cultivated dandelions which were grown as a salad crop.

Over the stokehole was the forcing house used mainly for seakale, chicory, endive and rhubarb. In another part of it were mushrooms. The manure for the mushrooms came direct from the stables: when a sufficiently large heap had been built up it was turned twice a day until sweet enough for bed making. Then as soon as its temperature dropped to the seventies the spawn, broken into pieces the size of a walnut, was put in. Finally when the mycelium was seen to be running, the manure was capped with soil and lime chippings and a few weeks later the mushrooms would appear.

The kitchen garden also had a fruit cage containing gooseberries, blackcurrants, raspberries and loganberries. Wire netting formed the outside of the cage and a net was thrown over the top as soon as the fruits began to open. One of my tasks was to go inside from time to time and push out any blackbirds that had managed to get in through tears or gaps in the netting.

As for top fruit, in front of our cottage on the estate was an orchard of close on two hundred trees. I got to know this orchard well while still a small boy for I would go through it to school and a few apples not only helped me on my way but formed a useful addition to the lunch I carried in my haversack. Thus, very early, I became aware of the different varieties. And, since then, whenever I have been brought an apple or pear to identify, I have looked at the eye of it and said to myself, 'Now, whereabouts in the orchard used that to be?' and almost always I have been able to come up with the answer and the name of the variety. It was a fine collection, planned to give a succession from August onwards. The first of the dessert apples to ripen were Beauty of Bath, Irish Peach and Worcester Pearmain, followed by Lady Sudeley, James Grieve, Rival and Wealthy. Other apples were Cox's Orange Pippin, King of the Pippins, Bismarck, Ellison's Orange, Dr Harvey, American Mother, Peasgood's Nonesuch, several russets and others. Codlins included Lord Suffield; cookers: Lord Derby, Lane's

Prince Albert, Bramley's Seedling, Newton Wonder, Mère de Ménage and Norfolk Beefing. Of the pears, if I remember rightly, the first to come was Jargonelle, the next William's Bon Chrétien. Then Louise Bonne of Jersey, Beurré Hardy, Beurré Superfin and Doyenne du Comice. For a young gardener this orchard provided a wonderful opportunity to learn the names of varieties.

The fruit was stored in an old coachhouse converted into a store. It was on the north side of a wall and in it apples would keep through until May or June, the last apples to emerge being usually Norfolk Beefing, Newton Wonder and Bramley's Seedling. The desserts had usually finished by then except perhaps for a few some-what shrivelled Cox's Orange Pippins.

Beyond the bottom end of the kitchen garden was marshy land; it had trees on it but to grow them it had been necessary to cut ditches to drain off the water into a stream some distance away. On this land while I was there it was decided to make a pond, a shrubbery and a home for primulas and bog plants. It was a big under-taking: the trees were pulled out by three-horse teams with chains and put on to timber waggons to be carted away. The pond had to be dug by hand with planks laid across the boggy land to take the wheelbarrows.

A big show was made with primulas. The first to flower was the variety Wanda on the rock garden. In the water garden were the species *rosea, denticulata, cashmiriana,* several varieties of *japonica* (one Father was particularly fond of was Red Hugh, which I haven't seen for years), the yellow *helodoxa,* followed by *pulver-ulenta* and *florindae,* the American cowslip. Late in the season I would be given the job of cutting off the seed-pods of the primulas, wrapping these in a square of matting and scattering them over the marshy areas of the woodland.

Many years later, at the time when I had become parks superintendent at Shrewsbury, I went back to Horwood House – which by then had been sold – into that woodland and gathered hundreds of seedlings of those primulas. They were of all kinds, well mixed up; I took them back with me and planted them in the Dingle at Shrewsbury where their descendants thrive today.

And I have many, too, by the poolside in my own garden.

Also planted were astilbes, *Iris sibirica* (a great bank of them to the side of the pond), bearded irises, peonies and others.

Some of the rarer plants at Horwood House came from Castle Kennedy, the home of the Earl of Stair near Stranraer in Wigtonshire, Scotland. The Dennys were friends of the Earl and often stayed with him. Outstanding among these plants was *Cardiocrinum giganteum* (*Lilium giganteum*) which grew in profusion at Castle Kennedy. They were huge! I remember gasping in astonishment the first time I saw the bulbs – nine to twelve inches across they were – when Father brought some back and gave them to me to plant in the bog garden. Then the waiting for them to flower – they flower once and then it means two to three years before the bulbils around are large enough to flower. Father collected the bulbils from the few bulbs he had and eventually finished up with a whole kitchen garden border of these gigantic lilies.

Other plants he brought back he was not always so

A flagged walk leading toward the house is flanked by mature herbaceous borders

The rock garden containing, among a host of other plants, some of the head gardener's favourite primulas

successful with. He perhaps forgot to take into account the fact that the Stranraer area of Scotland is kept unusually warm in winter by the Gulf Stream. He tried *Desfontainea spinosa,* a rather tender shrub from Peru and Chile looking something like a holly bush, and *Prostanthera violacea,* also an evergreen shrub, and neither was a success. And for years we struggled with rhododendrons and azaleas from Castle Kennedy but we had a limy soil and though we made special preparations the plants soon became sickly. (We had no iron sequestrene in those days with which to water them.) He did much better, however, with *Meconopsis baileyi* (*M. betonicifolia*) and built up a fine stock. By sowing the seed as soon as it was ripe he was able to achieve almost one hundred per cent. germination, but he found that if he kept it until the following spring the results were not nearly as good.

Father always prided himself on his begonias, especially the Gloire de Lorraine type and the hybrid winter-flowering ones such as Optima and Pink Beauty. Cyclamen was another favourite and he could produce plants eighteen to twenty-four inches across.

What of life apart from work in those days? Born in 1913, I have a hazy recollection of my father going off to enlist in the 1914–18 war but being turned down. I can also just recall the zeppelins over the village, the first German aeroplanes, the R100 airship stationed at Cardington not so far away and the R101 which was to come to a tragic end over France.

At Little Horwood church I was in the choir and later became a Sunday school teacher. We were expected to attend church regularly. Every Sunday Mr and Mrs Denny sat in their special place opposite the choir stalls and would look down into the church to see which members of the staff were present, or rather which members were absent.

The vicar was the Rev. Dunham. Many years later an elderly gentleman wearing a dog collar came up to me at the Royal Show and said, 'You don't remember me Percy?' I looked at him hard and recognized him as the vicar of my youth at Little Horwood. We began reminiscing and he told me that the very first time he had seen me was on a visit to Horwood House when Mr Denny and my father were taking him on a tour of the gardens. During the walk he had hinted that he would like some lettuce whereupon my father had turned to the little boy who was following behind and said: 'Percy, go to the south border and get a few lettuce plants and give them to the vicar'. I must have been about nine at the time.

And at the end of 1976 I was an invited speaker at a National Trust meeting when I met him again. He was eighty-seven, but full of life, and he introduced me to the audience, speaking of the old days at Little Horwood and saying how I had been a member of his church, his Sunsay school and the church school in the village. It brought back many memories.

Bulbs brought back from the garden of the Earl of Stair in Scotland produced these fine examples of *Cardiocrinum giganteum* (*Lilium giganteum*) in the kitchen garden at Horwood House

I took part in most of the activities of the village; I was in the cricket and football teams and I joined the Boy Scouts. I also threw a useful dart as a member of 'The Old Crown' dart team in matches with 'The Shoulder of Mutton', the other pub in Little Horwood, and with pubs in neighbouring villages.

I was influenced a good deal by my father: I admired what he did in the garden and in that respect he was my model. Yet he was very strict. For instance, the first time he caught me smoking (I was still at school) he gave me a good hiding. He wasn't to know that I had been smoking for some time before that! With Woodbines in those days five for twopence they weren't all that hard to come by and often I had a few puffs on the way back from school, chewing grass afterwards to get rid of the smell. My first encounter with a pipe stays in my memory. It came one evening when Father and Mother had gone to a whist drive and I was at home with one of my sisters. Father, who, like me in later years, was a confirmed pipe smoker, had a habit of filling a pipe and absentmindedly putting it back unsmoked in the pipe rack. On this evening I found such a full pipe and lighting up sank back in Father's chair feeling very much the grown-up man. But not for long. Soon I was turning green and making an urgent dash for the bathroom wanting to die. This did not stop me smoking, however; by the time I had left school I had tried beech leaves, dried dock leaves and various other substitutes for tobacco as well as continuing to have the occasional cigarette. I went on smoking cigarettes until the time came when I was saving up to get married and I found a pipe cheaper. I have smoked a pipe ever since and for 1972/3 the Briar Pipe Trade Association elected me runner-up for 'Pipe-man of the Year'.

At the time I began work in the gardens my father was smoking an ounce of tobacco a day. Every day he would send me to the village with a shilling for an ounce of St Julien and two boxes of matches. Only on a Saturday would he extend his purchase to two ounces and four boxes to last him the weekend.

As soon as I left school I decided to get a bicycle. I had wanted one sooner but Father said he couldn't afford it and that I must wait until I had the money myself. I wrote to Gamages for their catalogue and in it the bicycles were priced at fifty shillings each or half-a-crown a week on hire purchase. I ordered one on hire purchase. I had had it two months when Father saw me putting the weekly postal order in its envelope and asked what it was all about. I said, 'It's my half-a-crown for the bike'. He looked at me sternly and asked how much more I owed. I told him twenty-five shillings. He took out twenty-five shillings and handing the money to me said, 'That will finish your payments. You pay that off and never again have anything on hire purchase.' And I never have. But when it came later to me wanting a motor-bike he was adamant. 'If you ever have a motor-cycle,' he said, 'I'll see you out of that door.' He was against it because so many lads of my age were having accidents. And I never did have a motor-bike.

My basic wage being so low I naturally looked round for other ways of earning a few shillings. And there were always opportunities in the country.

For example, I could get sixpence for every mole I caught. I trapped them, cleaning out the burrows with a piece of wood and wearing gloves so that the moles would not catch the human smell. I put upturned turves around the traps to keep out the light, and soil over that. I would visit the traps after work, take out the dead moles and line them up at the bottom of the kitchen steps. At the end of a week I would tally them up and occasionally I would get more for catching moles than for my week's work.

And, of course, rabbits. The estate was full of them. We had many ways of catching them; one was to put netting round the warrens by the kitchen garden walls and drop a net over the top just before dusk – sometimes we caught forty to fifty rabbits in that fashion. I also snared rabbits. At other times we would go ferreting, using the ferret to drive the rabbits from their burrows so that we could shoot them. One had to be a fairly good shot for this as the rabbits would be out of one hole and into another like lightning followed by the ferret, so one had to be careful not to shoot the ferret instead of the rabbit. At harvest time we would be on the look-out for a binder working in a cornfield for we knew

Shooting: a lifelong hobby

it meant rabbits. We would get a stick and follow the binder and if luck was with us it could mean a rabbit to take home to Mother. What we liked most was to catch a three-quarter grown rabbit and get Mother to roast it. I was quite capable of eating the whole of such a rabbit just myself if it had been permitted, and if it were followed by rice pudding I would feel that life was especially good. I love rice pudding even today!

Shooting was one of my pastimes from an early age. When about seven I had a Diana airgun with which I would shoot at a penny or a matchbox on a gatepost. And I must only have been about twelve when being out with my father one day shooting rabbits he handed me the double-barrelled gun and two cartridges with a brief 'See what you can do'. I walked down to the bog garden, looked over the fence, took two shots and came back with two rabbits. It was a proud moment! A love of shooting has stayed with me ever since and is even today one of my main recreations.

Birds could also be profitable. For magpies and carrion crows the estate would pay sixpence a head, for they played havoc with the game. Blackbirds, rooks and sparrows did not bring in money but on the other hand all three were excellent for eating in pies. For sparrows we used a net between two long bamboo canes and put it over the ivy of the house or around the farm ricks. After dark we would shake the net and, if we heard a fluttering, bring the canes together and, with luck, ten or twelve sparrows would be caught. Two or three goes like this would provide sufficient for a fair-size pie. Not that Mother was overpleased when we brought them in. 'Dratted fiddling things' she called them, but nevertheless she would accept them and we would eagerly watch her cut and skin the tiny bodies and extract the two sides of the breasts to provide the makings of what was always, with a hard-boiled egg in the centre, the most delicious sparrow pie. Blackbirds we went after on moonlight nights in the winter when the hedges were leafless. We would find a blackbird sitting in the hedge and knock him down as he flew out. May was the month for rooks; and rook pie, too, was delicious. Alas, it is many years since I last tasted it.

23

Bees were kept to provide honey for the mansion and my father had charge of them. I helped him at times but unfortunately bees seem to dislike me, yet they never touched my father. He could go in among them without a veil, taking off the sections of honey and not being stung. Father, by the way, held the old country belief that if the owner of a hive died the bees of that hive must be told at once – a whisper was enough – or else they would take off and never return. The honey was put into jars by Mother and sent up to the House; the wax was

Feeding the pigeons, 1924

mixed with turpentine for floor polish. Mother also made a great deal of jam and bottled much fruit.

Horwood House was in the Whaddon Chase, well-known hunting country, and the Bicester and Grafton packs also hunted in the area. Foxes were almost a religion on the estate; we were not allowed into any of the coverts during the hunting season in case the foxes were disturbed and many a time I have sat on the top of the kitchen garden wall in the late evening and seen cubs playing and perhaps a vixen coming home with a rabbit or hen to feed them. Even before I had left school I followed the hounds at any opportunity. Not only was the hunt fascinating but I could also earn myself a few sixpences opening gates for the huntsmen. If the hunt came anywhere near the school, even if we were at lessons several of us lads would be up and away after it. It was well worth the caning we got for so doing. Today it still stirs me to hear the huntsman's horn or the hounds in full cry. I know much is said about cruelty to the fox but I was brought up in a hunting district and I don't think it is as cruel as many people try to make out. True, the fox is hunted by a pack of hounds and by men and women on horseback, but the fox is a sight more crafty than the majority of hounds and ninety-nine times out of a hundred he will outwit them.

Hunting was the main sport of the Dennys. Mr Denny, his son and his daughters all took part and they kept a string of six or seven top class hunters with a head groom and three undergrooms to look after them. Mr Denny himself was a great lover of horses and a notable shot. He was also squire and lay rector of Little Horwood.

The hunt took precedence over almost everything. I recall once how the fox came into the kitchen garden and my father shut the doors to keep the hounds from entering and trampling over his carefully cultivated garden. But Mr Denny would have none of it; in fact he was furious at the hounds being kept out. He opened the doors himself and let them in, whereupon they proceeded to ruin most of the seedbeds and much else besides. What Father said about the hounds that day is nobody's business!

Dancing was one of our favourite pastimes. In my

25

biking days we would go to dances at Little Horwood, Great Horwood, a mile or so away, Swanbourne, Mursley and several other villages within ten miles or so of home. If we met a girl we liked at the dance we would offer her a lift back on the step of the bicycle. One foot on the step, her knee on the carrier, her hands on our shoulders – that is the way we took our girls home in those days. One of the reasons why we wanted motor-bikes was that the pillion seat was so much more comfortable and therefore so much more of an attraction to the girls.

The village hall at Little Horwood was owned by the estate and dances were held in it most weeks – the first dance I ever did there was the Charleston.

Another dance that sticks in my memory was at the Oddfellows Hall in Winslow our nearest town. Four or five of us cycled over and we bought a five-shilling bottle of Sandeman's port which we supped before we went along to the dance. But when we arrived at the Hall the whist drive which preceded the dance had not finished. So I went to the nearest pub and drank some beer. On top of the port it had a very potent effect and when I eventually started dancing the room began to spin round. I had enough sense to get out quickly and I finished up in somebody's yard, sitting in an old farm cart. And was I ill! Later I staggered back to the dance and the first person I met was my Sunday school teacher. Luckily I managed to pull myself together and act fairly normally. All my friends thought it a great joke!

Another occasion on which I misbehaved myself was one Guy Fawkes Night. We had gone over to Mursley, the adjoining village, with our fireworks and I threw a Jumping Jack in the midst of a gang of girls who were standing around talking. They screamed and ran and I felt proud of my effort until suddenly a heavy hand fell on my shoulder and looking up I saw it was the village bobby. He charged me with letting off fireworks on the carriage highway and took my name and address. I had to tell Father when I got home and I received a good hiding from him. My friends kept telling me that I would either go to jail or pay a heavy fine but when I eventually appeared in court I was let off with a warning. But it cured me of throwing fireworks at girls, and my crime sheet is still clean!

Every year at the House was held the Servants' Ball when the house was thrown open to the staff, drinks and food and a band were provided free and we young men were able to seek out and dance with our favourite parlourmaid, housemaid, kitchenmaid or whoever else we fancied. The Dennys would come in for the first hour of the dance but then leave us on our own.

Christmas was also a great time there. The gardeners would be busy making chains of evergreens to go round the big rooms. Then the Christmas tree had to be prepared and taken in for the young Dennys to do the decorations. There would be presents for all of us from the Dennys. At Christmas, too, a party would be given for the children from the village, and we were included; and many little extras of food and so on were given to the staff.

Though things have changed a great deal during my lifetime I still take my mind back to those days in the gardens of a private estate. The life was cried down by many; we were slaves, some people said. Our wages certainly were not large; mine were six shillings, an ordinary gardener got twenty-eight shillings and my father, I think, received £2 a week. But on top of that we had a free house, free light (the electricity was generated on the estate), free milk, vegetables and fruit and often a joint of meat from the estate farm. And whenever the Dennys came back from shooting we could be pretty sure of a brace of grouse or pheasant, and often after they had been deer stalking a large lump of venison would come our way.

Above all it was a community. Inside the house were the butler, footman, head parlourmaid, assistant parlour-maid, head housemaid and three under-maids. In the kitchen were the cook, kitchen maid and two maids under her. The between-maid went between the various departments. Two ladies' maids looked after Mrs Denny and the daughters. Outside were the chauffeur, assistant chauffeur, electrician, head groom, under-grooms, head gardener, farm bailiff and their staffs.

For youngsters like ourselves living in a small village

the choice of occupation was very limited. A lad went into farming, gardening, grooming, chauffeuring: little else. Girls entered service as housemaid, kitchenmaid or parlourmaid. The elder of my two sisters went into Horwood House as housemaid for several years until she married a local farmer. (Later they sold the farm and took 'The Crown' public house at Great Horwood, then an hotel at Verney Junction and in recent years they have been running a thriving florist and greengrocery business at Buckingham.) The other sister started as kitchenmaid, moving up to parlourmaid. She, too, left when she got married, in her case to a bookmaker from Winslow where they still live.

Both my brothers began in the gardens the same as me. Harry, the eldest, gave it up to become first a pantryboy under the butler at Horwood House, then a footman at Horwood and at the Denny's London house in Grosvenor Street. Eventually he left and was footman to the head-master of Harrow School for a while. He never married and spent his whole life until retirement as a gentleman's servant, finishing as a butler. My younger brother, Maurice, also began in the garden but this was after I had left. He soon found that more money was to be earned with a contracting firm that was laying a water main in the district so he left. Later he went into the greengrocery business.

Nobody had much money with which to go out regularly, so a good deal of our entertainment was at home. Mother made wine: dandelion, cowslip, rose petal, celery, mangold, wheat, raisin, potato, elderflower, elderberry; these were some of them. The wine was put into five-gallon casks and at the end of a year or so Mother would bottle it off and stack it on the shelves of an outside larder, each bottle marked with the name and year. The elderberry would come out when we had colds – heated on the range with ginger added, a tot of that sweated away any cold. Other wines made an appearance when we had visitors, which was quite often, for on the estate we visited each other's house regularly. One evening possibly the butler, head groom, electrician, chauffeur and farm bailiff, and usually their wives as well if they were married, might look in at our place and

The Throwers picnicking with Mr Brudenell (the stationmaster at Swanbourne) and his family. The author is seated on the far left

spend a few hours sampling Mother's wine. Then perhaps the next night it would be somebody else's place and Mother and Father would be among the visitors. And however potent the wine (and believe me, some of it certainly was) no one had far to stagger home when the evening was over.

Holidays were rare treats. There was the occasional Sunday school outing. One, I remember, was to Southend and my companion on that trip was Bill Sharp who worked with me in the gardens. At Southend we decided to take out a rowing boat and we went too far and were caught up in the wake of a passing steamer and nearly drowned. I couldn't swim at that time and it was touch and go for a while. When Father and Mother heard about it they played merry hell, for as both of them had been born by the sea they knew the perils far better than I did.

Another seaside holiday was when Mother took me for a week to her parents' home at Walberswick. We went by train and I recollect being taken round Walberswick by pony and trap to see the huge bomb craters caused by the shelling from German warships in the 1914–18 war. Grandfather Dunnett made a big impression on my young mind. He was a strong, big, bearded man who lived mainly by fishing. I say mainly for I have my suspicions that he made a bit in other ways. I discovered that in his cottage where we were staying one of the rooms had a false floor and under it were stacked casks of spirits which, so I was told, had been washed ashore from wrecks and of which the Customs were certainly not aware! Every now and again Grandfather would have his cronies in, lock the doors and get down to a good drinking session. Grandfather owned a black Labrador dog which he took with him shooting on the marshes; any duck he brought down the dog would be after like a flash and bring it back. From that time onwards I always wanted to own a black Labrador.

The time came when I had served four years in the gardens at Horwood House and one day my father said, 'If you want to get on in gardening you've got to leave here. You must go to other gardens . . . move about to other parts of the country to get experience with different conditions. Where would you like to go?'

29

I said I didn't know, which was true for I hadn't given it much thought, though several of the other lads had moved on to places such as Waddesdon Manor, Tring Park, King's Waldenbury and Luton Hoo. So I asked him where *he* thought I should go, but I certainly never expected the answer he gave me. It was: 'What would you think about the Royal Gardens at Windsor?' Windsor was one of the top places in the country and I hadn't even considered it. I remember saying something like, 'Oh, by gum, that would be nice', and the next I knew he had written to C. H. Cook the head gardener at Windsor (he had probably met him at shows) saying he had a son keen on gardening and was there possibly an opening.

He must have told a good story for back came a letter offering me a position in the Royal Gardens as an improver at £1 a week.

Showing me the letter my father said, 'You realize that if you take the job you'll have to live in a bothy?' I knew what a bothy was; we had a small one at Horwood House with five lads in it next door to our cottage and I quite fancied the idea of living in one. I decided to go to Windsor.

The étang with its enormous water lilies and impressive standard fuchsias

Royal Bothy Days

The fact that the head gardener's son was going away to work in the Royal Gardens impressed Mrs Denny so much that she instructed a chauffeur to take Father and myself to Windsor in one of the Horwood House cars. So we arrived in style.

We went first to the head gardener's house. The door was answered by a large man wearing what I later came to recognize as almost a badge of office, a bowler hat. He greeted Father, looked down as if to say 'What are you?' and then proceeded more or less to ignore me.

I was taken to the bothy, which was to be my home for the next four and a half years; Father said goodbye and I was on my own for the first time in my life.

At that time, 1931, Windsor Royal Gardens had over sixty gardeners though the staff was already beginning to be cut back because of rising costs. The bothy was the home for about twenty men, mostly young improvers like myself but also a few disabled ex-servicemen who did odd jobs about the garden. A large building with two wings, the bothy was reputed to be the finest in the country. It was certainly good. Each of us had his own bedroom, there was a dining room, kitchen and billiard room and we were even provided with a wireless. A woman came in every morning to do the cleaning and cook the breakfast and midday meal but at other times, including weekends, we had to look after ourselves.

One of the first persons I met was the bothy caterer. 'Meat, vegetables and milk are supplied by us free,' he informed me, 'but you'll pay for things like butter, jam, sugar and bread. Those you buy off me and settle up at the end of the week when I make up my accounts. So my advice to you is to go as easy as possible on them or you'll find they make quite a big hole in your wages'. I ate normally for the first week and the account with the bothy caterer came to nine shillings which, out of my wage of twenty shillings, wasn't too bad. Certainly I had more money left than with the six shillings I had been getting at Horwood House even though I was now living away from home and also was not in a position to benefit from the perks such as catching moles and rabbits. And, what is more, after I had been at Windsor a week they put my money up by a whole shilling!

Anyway, having left home I felt much more grown up, and living in a bothy soon made me more independent and better able to look after myself. I learnt to make my own bed, to cook, to wash up and even to darn my socks. (Though my wife doesn't seem to rate my abilities in these fields quite as highly as I do myself! I will admit my darning is not quite up to standard – it was always more of a cobble than a darn and the result could be quite painful to walk on.)

Right away I made up my mind that I wouldn't go to Father or Mother for anything. I was determined to be independent. Father did now and again send me a few shillings to help out but I never asked for it. It was quite hard going at times. Often I would get back to the bothy after a dance or perhaps having had a couple of drinks at the local 'Lord Nelson' pub to find that I was broke until the end of the week. I used to think, 'Heavens, if anything happened at home, what would I do?' and as soon as I was able I tried to have at least a ten-shilling note tucked away in case of emergency. I also learnt ways of economizing such as buying New Zealand butter instead of English (it was a penny a pound cheaper) and making a good meal out of half a pound of sausages and bread and butter.

The order of garden seniority at Windsor was head gardener, foreman (five in various departments), specialist grower, journeyman and improver. Charles (C.H.) Cook was the head gardener; he was a man destined to become very important in my life and I will have much more to say about him later. Foremen I remember were Dickson, outside; Palmer, kitchen garden; Waltham, fruit; Hale, plants; Hubbard, pleasure grounds. The two I was to see most of were Waltham and Hale.

The gardener's lad arrived at Windsor in style: in a chauffeur-driven car

The bothy at Windsor

32

The three specialist growers were Hobday, orchids; Jeffries, chrysanthemums; and Pascoe, carnations. These foremen and specialist growers were all important men; their jobs in the Royal Gardens were as responsible and well paid as those of most head gardeners on private estates. And that being so, they rarely bothered to move on from Windsor, particularly as when they retired they were assured of a pension and a house to live in.

Each foreman had his own separate department with its own tools, equipment, compost, pots and so on. And these things were jealously guarded: anything borrowed had to be returned promptly to the appropriate foreman and put back in its correct place.

Of those that lived in the bothy I cannot remember all the names, for over the four and a half years I was there many left and others came. Those I still recall readily after over forty-five years (can it really be as long ago as that?) are Fred Newman, Ted Sturgess, Bob Musk, Jimmy Smith (he finished up as parks superintendent at Cheltenham), Tom Holt, Bill Shapland, Tommy Miles, Sydney Turner, Leonard Dando, Jack Hughes and Archie Starks. But there were many others. Of the ex-servicemen living in the bothy the two I remember most clearly were Leo Brown and his brother Charlie. Leo had lost a leg in the 1914–18 war and in memory I can still hear him swearing of a morning in his room as he strapped on his artificial limb. Both brothers did odd jobs in the gardens. The Royals were very good to any of their staff who suffered in the war, always finding something for them to do while paying full wages. Several crippled soldiers were lodgekeepers.

We were certainly a mixed crowd but on the whole we got on well together, hard work and a shortage of money tending to keep us out of mischief. It was difficult to get together enough money to spend on drink though we did have a Scotsman among us (he is in the list above but I won't mention his name!) who would stay in the bothy for about six weeks without ever going out, saving his money. Then suddenly he would break out and it would be every night for perhaps a week with him coming back three sheets in the wind. Then it was back to the confined, sober life of the bothy for another six weeks.

33

Bothy boys, by the way, were not allowed to get married. If you did you were finished; you had to find a job where there was a cottage. Which reminds me of a friend of mine in the bothy who was going round the greenhouses at Windsor one night when a white barn owl flew down in front of him and out through one of the ventilators. He told the foreman about it next morning and the foreman said in a serious voice, 'Sign of a birth, that is'. We all tittered at this. But about a month later my friend came – almost on his hands and knees – to the foreman to inform him that he had to get married and would have to leave. Even today whenever an owl flies across the headlights of my car I tend automatically to turn to my passenger and say, 'Sign of a birth that'.

An improver like me in the early days at Windsor followed the journeyman around doing the cleaning up after him and assisting generally. The journeyman was in charge and did the more responsible tasks, for example tying down, stopping and thinning vines. The journeyman, in turn, was not allowed to encroach on the prerogatives of the specialist grower.

We young gardeners had to turn up each morning washed, shaved and looking respectable. We wore a blue baize apron which we had to buy ourselves and in its pocket we carried a knife which was provided for us. The journeymen were also given budding knives. The knives were honed on a whetstone and the test for sharpness was to run it over the back of the hand – if it shaved off the hairs without any trouble it was sharp enough.

We started off our day at 6.30 am by watering, picking over and removing dead or yellow leaves and fading flowers, swilling down the greenhouses, scrubbing them out and leaving everything in perfect order. Every man had his set job from the time he started and he had to stick to it until it was finished.

We bothy boys took it in turns to do duty roster. This meant being confined to the gardens during the evenings and weekends and having to attend to all the routine tasks such as watering, damping down and adjustments to the ventilation. We read the thermometers at regular intervals, using a hurricane lantern if it were dark. Adjusting the ventilation to raise or lower the temperature was not the

Harry Thrower with Waltham, the foreman of the fruit section at Windsor. The two had worked together previously in the gardens at Kings Waldenbury

comparatively simple job it is today with automatic equipment. The ventilators in the large fruit range at Windsor, for example, were massive affairs that slid over the roof, each on a chain. They took so long to adjust that it could happen that by the time the duty man had gone round opening them, the climatic conditions had changed and he would have to go back over all of them again, closing them up. We did not have to bother with the boilers though, for there were three men, each doing an eight-hour shift, to attend to them. But we would report to the stokers if the temperature was down in any house or the heating was not correct.

My first foreman was Waltham who, as it turned out, had been at King's Waldenbury with my father, Waltham inside foreman, Father outside. He was in charge of the Royal Garden fruit houses which comprised greenhouses for cucumbers, melons and strawberries together with two fruit ranges, each a quarter of a mile long which, divided into four, served the four seasons of the year. The ranges also had corridors: one with figs, another with apricots, a third with plums. The early range held peaches and nectarines growing in pots, early grapes (Black Hamburgh and Foster's Seedling), two more strawberry houses, more peaches and nectarines on the walls and another vinery where the grapes ripened later. This early range had to provide ripe strawberries for when the Court came to Windsor Castle from Buckingham Palace at Eastertime and those in charge were also responsible for ensuring that grapes, both black and white, peaches and nectarines were ready and at their best by May 26th, Queen Mary's birthday. The other range produced the later fruit: peaches (Peregrine, Duke of York, Hale's Early); nectarines (Humboldt, Pine Apple, Lord Napier) and grapes (Muscat of Alexandria, Alicante, Madresfield Court and Mrs Pince).

To begin with I was not allowed to do a thing on my own. Whatever it was, watering, stopping, topdressing, ventilating – Waltham was there to show me exactly how it was done. But the next time I was given that particular job if it wasn't done in the way he had told me I was in for a severe dressing down.

After a spell in the cucumber and melon houses I

moved to the early fruit range and then to the later one. I learnt to recognize the different varieties of greenhouse fruit not only by sight but also by taste. For, although we were not allowed to pick the fruit for ourselves, anything which fell to the ground we could take back for the bothy. And I suppose, we being young, a few fruits may have fallen to the ground before nature really intended them to! But we certainly got to know which were the best flavoured fruits – something again that was to prove useful to me for the rest of my gardening life.

Another important place was the orchard house. This was a large unheated building containing extra-large clay pots in which were grown peaches, nectarines, cherries, plums, apples, pears and other fruit. The fruit from those pot-grown trees could be superb. The cherries, for example; I have never tasted any with their flavour before or since. And the peaches, nectarines and apples were always a wonderful colour. But this orchard house culture involved a good deal of hard work especially in the wintertime when we had to take each of these heavy pots and, with a pointed stick, tease out the soil from around and between the tree roots to leave two inches of space between the side of the pot and the root ball. Often the root balls were so solid that the effort of getting the soil out would take the skin off the side of our hands. Another time-consuming task was watering these pots in summer: when it was really hot it needed doing every day.

Liquid manure was much used at Windsor. Near where we kept the horses for the garden and the head gardener had a few pigs and poultry, stood the manure heap, regularly replenished with manure from the stables. Beside it was a pit in which the liquid was collected. One of our regular jobs was to fill a wooden barrel on wheels with the liquid manure and take it to the fruit ranges where it was applied to the trees at the rate of one part to three parts water. The water we used was Thames water pumped from the river and, believe me, it was something quite different from mains water. Leave a hose with Thames water in it overnight and the first water out of it the next morning would stink like a sewage farm. Goodness knows what was in it! But it was effective stuff and I am sure it had a lot to do with the magnificent quality of the fruit at Windsor, coupled, of course, with plenty of hard work.

Waltham was a strict taskmaster and would not stand for any slovenly work, as I found out to my cost when he first entrusted me with the task of tying in a fan-trained peach tree. In fan training the lower branches have to start at the bottom of the wall absolutely horizontal and the remainder of the branches are arranged like the spokes of a fan at equal intervals but at a slight angle. It can take a whole day to tie in just one tree. The first time I was put on this job, I had almost finished when Waltham came along to see how I was doing. He stood back, took a long look and quietly uttered three words. They were: 'That won't do'. He then took out his knife and cut every tie I had made. I had to start all over again, and I daren't utter a single word of protest.

Waltham – just like my father – would not allow me to do any pruning at all (even after I had been promoted to journeyman gardener). In his opinion (but not in mine, though in hindsight, perhaps he was right!) I hadn't sufficient knowledge to know which branches to cut and which to leave alone. So he pruned and I followed doing the tying up.

Potting of strawberries to get them ripe for Easter was one of Waltham's specialities. We made the compost a cartload at a time – a cartload being twelve barrowloads and a barrowload twelve shovelfuls. It was made up of three parts soil, two parts leafmould, one part decayed manure plus a five-inch pot of bonemeal and a similar amount of La Fruitier fertilizer (from William Wood of Taplow) to every barrowload. The manure was cow manure put under a greenhouse bench to dry out ready for breaking up with a hammer and putting through a quarter-inch riddle. While we were potting Waltham would be backwards and forwards timing us to see how many pots we were doing to the hour. From time to time he would pick up a potted strawberry; press the soil with his huge thumb and if he made an impression he would tip it out and make us do it again. But though Waltham tested our work by pressing with his thumb he would never allow us to use our thumbs for potting.

He had a wooden pot rammer and if he saw one of us with our thumbs in a pot he would bring his rammer across the knuckles of the culprit who seldom forgot the lesson.

At other times I spent many long hours on the top of a step-ladder thinning grapes. It was very warm in those vineries and the sweat would run off the tip of my nose. We were not allowed to touch a berry with our fingers but had to use a forked stick and long grape scissors with sharp points. Once started we had to continue until the thinning was finished. Another long wearisome task was brushing the vines with methylated spirit to get rid of mealy bug. So was tying down the shoots with raffia for it had to be attended to every day in the growing season. And if we so much as cracked one shoot we were for it.

Ants were a serious pest at Windsor. Not the ordinary ant but the Argentine species which had been introduced on some plants from South America. They were everywhere. My first encounter with them was on my second day at Windsor and our meeting place was in the bothy. I had arrived on a Saturday and been given my sugar and jam which I had put in the cupboard allocated to me, and on the Sunday morning went to get them out for breakfast. Opening the cupboard door I got the shock of my life! I just couldn't see sugar or jam for ants! Not only were they all over the food but a solid mass covered the leg of the table under the cupboard and a broad procession was making its way across the floor to the door. After that experience I kept my food in sealed jars. Our communal meat (this included venison sent into the bothy from Windsor Great Park) was another target of these ants and we had to take a tray of water, stand empty jam jars upright in it and lay the meat over the top of these in order to keep it safe.

The ants were also a serious problem in the gardens and although the Office of Works and other experts were called in, no one found a completely successful solution. Mr Cook's own method was to soak cottonwool with nicotine (he used the old XL All insecticide which was 90 per cent. or so pure nicotine) and put it on a large plate which he left at the bottom of a doorpost in a greenhouse. Next morning the plate would be completely

Climbers and flowering pot plants decorate the plant corridors at Windsor

hidden under a pile of dead ants and, as ants always go back for their dead, for the next two or three days a stream of ants would be seen going to and fro taking their comrades' bodies away for burial, or whatever ants do with their dead. Ants could be particularly troublesome when we were watering the vineries for they emerged from the borders, as the water soaked in, and swarmed up the glass of the vinery almost blocking out the daylight. What we did was to put soft soap into warm water, mix it up with a syringe, add half a cupful of paraffin and when the mixture turned milky spray it over the ants. This was quite effective. The ants were a worry, too, in that they carried the mealy bug around, which, I think, was the main reason why mealy bug was always a serious pest at Windsor. Ants seem to enjoy eating the honeydew of the mealy bug as much as they do that of the greenfly.

Another feature of the fruit section at Windsor was the grape house, a thatched building with varnished pine-panelled rooms where bunches of grapes were stored. The grape house was full of bottles of water each holding a bunch of grapes cut with a length of bare stem to take up the water. The favourite variety for storing thus was Alicante and I have known these to be in top condition until Christmas and even well into the New Year. These out-of-season grapes were sent to Windsor Castle, Buckingham Palace or perhaps some other royal establishment if requested.

Our gardens at Windsor were also expected to supply other special fruits which would be sent to, say, Buckingham Palace, Cowes, Balmoral, and occasionally to Sandringham, though Sandringham did grow their own fruit and only required special out-of-season produce from us.

Grapes, figs, peaches, nectarines, apricots and so on all had their specially designed containers and when packing these we had to be very gentle in handling the fruit: if as much as a fingermark was found on a peach for instance, we were for it.

This training I had in the fruit houses at Windsor was of a kind that, since those days, it has been almost impossible for a young gardener to obtain. For to grow fruit under glass is an art in itself. In all things we were taught to do the right thing, at the right time: no half measures. And this strict training both at Windsor and Horwood has stood me in good stead in the years since. We had to do our work properly; if we didn't we were out, and if one were sacked from a private estate in those days it meant leaving without a reference and consequently having little chance of getting a similar position anywhere else in private service. Speaking for myself the one thing I worried about more than anything in those early days was the fear of getting the sack. Thankfully it never happened.

After two years in fruit I was moved to the plant houses where I was put in charge of the stove house, show house, corridor and all the growing houses with the exception of those for orchids, carnations and chrysanthemums which were in the care of the specialist growers.

The main show house had bougainvilleas and other climbers including a rare one with petals like crêpe paper whose name I had forgotten until I saw it again in Madeira recently and recognized it as *Lagerstroemia indica*. All these climbers had to be pruned back and trained during the winter months when the house was left open with just sufficient heat to keep the frost at bay. By Ascot Week in June when the Court arrived at Windsor this show house would be filled with hydrangeas. Leading out from the show house was a corridor with tall fuchsias on either side: a truly fine sight. It was these magnificent specimens at Windsor that began my lifelong love for fuchsias and I still grow some of the varieties which made up that corridor – Brutus, Mrs Marshall, Marinka, Mrs Pearson, to mention only a few. This corridor led into what was called the lounge, a large greenhouse with seats and groups of plants placed round about for decorative effect. There were clivias and arum lilies, *Cestrum elegans* with its lovely pendent reddish flowers and the climbing rose Maréchal Niel (one of the best of its kind, beautifully scented). I recall *Plumbago capensis* (the blue one), *Prostanthera violacea*, an outstanding callistemon (we called it metrosideros in those days), acacia, the large ficus and a host of others. The lounge was tiled and every morning it had to be

The Dingle, Shrewsbury

Below

The Range of Glasshouses at The Royal Gardens, Windsor. From the
catalogue of Mackenzie and Moncur Ltd., who erected the range: 'This
extensive block of houses, probably the largest private range in the world,
comprises the following houses: 14 Vineries, 8 Peach Houses, 3 Fig
Houses, 2 Palm Houses, 6 Orchid Houses, 2 Show Malmaison Houses,
2 Carnation Houses, 2 Flowering Show Houses, Tropical House, Laelia
House, 2 Propagating Houses, Stove Houses, 2 Cypripedium Houses,
2 Dendrobium Houses, Begonia House, 2 Cyclamen Houses, 2 Geranium
Houses, 3 Azalea Houses, Fernery, 2 Amaryllis Houses, 4 Cucumber
Houses, 4 Melon Houses, 2 Tomato Houses, 2 Eucharis Houses,
2 Imantophyllum Houses, 2 Pelargonium Houses, Rose House,
2 Connecting Plant Corridors, also Gardeners' Quarters Cottages, Back
Offices, Stables, Cart-sheds, Workshops etc.
The statistically-minded may be interested to know that 44,000 cubic feet
of teakwood were used in the hothouses, over 156,000 superficial feet of
glass were used, and the heating pipes total 11 miles.'

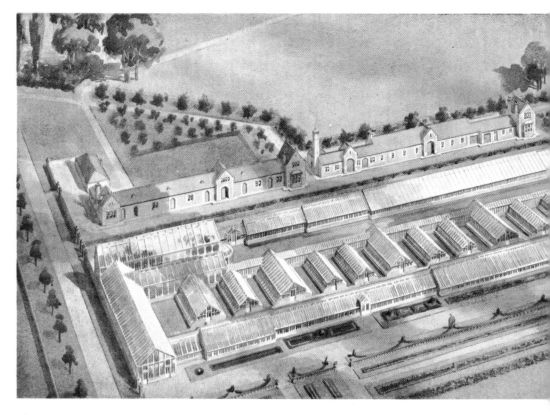

C. H. Cook, head gardener in
The Royal Gardens, Windsor
from 1924 to 1936

swept, swilled down with a hosepipe and left spotless with not even a dead leaf to be seen.

My foreman in the plant houses was Norman Hale, a short bouncy man with a long moustache. He wore a bowler hat gone green with age and would stand no nonsense from anyone. He was a great character. I shall never forget the day when one of the bothy lads reported for duty holding his side. The lad (it wasn't me!) was a big, soft sort of a chap who always had something wrong with him. Hale never had much time for him and on this occasion enquired bluntly:

'What's the matter with you then this morning?'

'Oh, Gawd! I've got such a pain here,' said the lad clutching his side.

Hale looked at him with a serious face, seemed to consider for several moments then announced, 'I think it's a tubrick you've got, my lad.'

'Tubrick?' he groaned alarmed, 'what's that, Mr Hale, what's that?'

We all awaited the answer with interest.

'It's confused wind,' Hale replied slowly, 'your face is so much like your backside that the wind don't know which way to turn!'

The growing houses I looked after had to provide a succession of flowers for decoration throughout the whole year. In the early part of the year we would have amaryllis in flower, cinerarias, large-flowered calceolarias, schizanthus, stocks in pots, salpiglossis, clarkia and godetia in the show house and along the corridor for the benefit of the royal owners and their visitors. Then came hydrangeas, fuchsias, geraniums, pelargoniums and so on and in the winter, cyclamen and the various primulas – *malacoides, kewensis, sinensis, obconica* – to give continuity for the whole twelve months. Other flowers came from the orchid, chrysanthemum and carnation houses. In the west house which had wooden lath blinds for shading, gardenias were grown, and gardenias were extremely important at Windsor for we had to have a gardenia *every* morning of the year to put on King George V's breakfast table for him to pick up and put in his buttonhole when he had finished eating. There was no argument about it: a gardenia *had* to be on that table!

Part of The English Garden in Berlin

45

We also had to supply bedding plants for places such as the east terrace of Windsor Castle, at Frogmore and at the Mausoleum. And we always had to bear in mind the likes and dislikes of the King and Queen. For one thing Queen Mary would not have any hard colours in the flower schemes. She insisted always on pastel shades, pale blues and, for preference, pinks. She wouldn't have a red Paul Crampel geranium at any price, but would be very happy with the pale pink Mrs Lawrence (which I still use myself today). Her fuchsias must not be too bright and for lobelias she liked pale blue. Also plenty of silvery foliage plants. Today one of my own favourite schemes for bedding remains pale pink, silver and blue; and I am sure that dates back to the time when those were the royal preferences and the east terrace of Windsor Castle in particular was a splendid mass of these quiet-coloured plants.

Of course it wasn't all work at Windsor. We young men of the bothy had our fun. When we went out at night we were supposed to take a key, for all the gates were locked at ten o'clock. But many a time I have been out without one and had to throw a coat over the spikes of the railings and climb in that way. Sometimes we

The head gardener's house at Windsor befitted the dignity of the position

would cycle to the Lodge, leave our bicycles and go into Windsor town for some form of entertainment. At other times we went to dances round about. We drank, I remember, old and mild – a good drink – three or four of those and we could do any dance that the band could play! And it also gave the courage to ask a girl to dance. But one thing we were warned right from the start; that was, 'Keep your eyes off the head gardener's daughters.' For the head gardener had two attractive daughters, Connie and Mabel.

The head gardener himself, C. H. Cook (he was Charles to his friends but we wouldn't have dared to call him by his Christian name) was quite a formidable character. He was in the top rank of gardeners, having come from Lord Derby's estate at Knowsley in Lancashire and before that had been with the Duke of Buccleuch at Dalkeith in Midlothian. He was one of four famous gardening brothers: Tom was head gardener to the Royal Family at Sandringham, Sam head gardener for the Cadbury family and Harry (H. H.) head gardener at Reading University. Their father had been a head gardener at Kilshayne in Ireland.

It was the heyday of big gardening names with men such as Barnes at Eton Hall, Puddle at Bodnant, Johnson at Waddesdon Manor, Metcalfe at Luton Hoo, Lindacres at Mentmore, Roland Smith at Weston Hall, Tom Hay (father of Roy) at Hyde Park, and so on.

Like all the head gardeners on large estates C. H. Cook was a gentleman in his own right. Dressed in black jacket, pinstripe trousers and bowler hat he would pace through the gardens with the dignity of any lord. His day started at 8.30 of a morning when he began his walk around. He was so regular that we could usually work out just when he would reach the particular place where we happened to be working and be very busy when he passed. But he knew all the tricks. Every now and again he would go past but return a few minutes later. And woe betide the gardener who had slackened off or was fooling around! Cook had eyes like a hawk and we were perpetually worried in case he perhaps saw a fruit tree not tied in properly, a plant that needed water or a house that hadn't been damped down properly. He was

certainly monarch of all he surveyed as far as the gardens were concerned. But though a strict man we had to acknowledge that he was a fair one. His house was in the centre of the greenhouse area and one thing he always watched for was the time we finished. We could stop right on the dot – as long as we didn't leave anything unfinished. For the one thing he expected of his staff was that they would finish off a task even if it took them ten minutes of their own time.

(This is one complaint I have today. I've had men potting up a batch of plants and when knocking-off time comes they may have five plants still to pot up. Will they stay and finish them so that the job is done and they can make a clean start the next morning? Oh, no, they must stop dead on time no matter what the situation. This was one thing we were taught never to do.)

I remember an encounter with Mr Cook one day when I was working in a vinery. Smoking was strictly forbidden while we were working and usually we slipped off to the toilets every now and again for 'two draws and a spit'. But on this occasion all the windows of the vinery were wide open (the vines were resting and I was cleaning them up and giving them a tar oil wash) so I decided to risk it and have a quick smoke inside. I had been to a dance the night before and was dying for a smoke. All went well and nobody saw me. Then about an hour later Mr Cook came along with a visitor, a man called Phillips who had once been a journeyman-gardener at Windsor and was now in charge of the cemeteries at Slough. I heard their steps over the iron grating which covered the hot water pipes and I carried on busily working. As soon as Mr Cook came into the part where I was, out of the corner of my eye I saw him put his nose in the air and sniff. He was, by the way, a non-smoker. Then he spoke. 'Thrower,' he said, in a quiet voice, 'someone been fumigating with nicotine in here?' He didn't wait for me to answer but walked on through with his friend. I felt about as small as a sixpence and could willingly have fallen through the grating.

Another time I was on bothy duty and had sneaked out into the town for something or other. When on duty we were not allowed to leave the place under any pretext unless we found someone to relieve us. Someone had to be in the bothy to deal with any exigency that arose. We did a week's duty at a time and on one night would have an official relief. But on this occasion things were quiet and I had slipped out for a short while without leaving a relief. Cook saw me in the town and gave me a lift back. I was very worried that he would ask me if I were on duty, but he said nothing. Next morning, however, he came round on his tour of the greenhouses and when he reached me said, 'Thrower . . . you're on duty this week, are you not?' 'Yes, sir' I replied apprehensively. 'Then what were you doing in the town last night?' and he proceeded to give me a real good telling off for deserting my post.

But to go back to the daughters. I became very attracted to Mr Cook's daughter Connie who when I first arrived at Windsor was still at the High School. Then she went to work for W. H. Smith's in Windsor and she used to cycle through the gardens and I would be up at the top greenhouse of a morning to wave to her as she went by. Then she changed her job and went with the Westminster Bank at Slough, but still continued to cycle through the gardens and often after leaving work at 5.30 I would make my way through Windsor Great Park to meet her. And when I was on duty of a night-time I would eagerly look in the windows of the Cook's house to see if she were about: sometimes when her parents were busy in the lounge she would talk to me through the kitchen window.

Then we began walking back together from Windsor Parish Church of a Sunday evening. If not on duty the bothy boys were expected to attend church at least once on a Sunday. Mr and Mrs Cook went in the morning with their two daughters, but Connie would go again in the evening on her own, and we would stroll back through the Long Walk and into the grounds so far . . . and then I would have to leave her to go the rest of the way on her own. Our courtship went on from there but all the time we had to meet on the sly for fear her father might have me moved if he got to hear about our friendship.

Now and again we would sneak off to the pictures: the first film I took her to see was Gracie Fields in *Sally* at the Windsor Cinema. In the summer Connie and her sister would go for a walk down to the bottom of the Park and I would take a different route to meet them 'accidentally' along by the river! We also looked forward each year to the annual dance in aid of the Gardeners' Royal Benevolent Society which was organized by the Cooks and the bothy boys were invited. If I were lucky I would have several dances with Connie despite her father keeping his eye on her. And that is how things were with us during my stay at Windsor.

Mr Cook always escorted royalty and other visitors around the gardens. Queen Mary was a keen gardener and she and King George would walk through the greenhouses, plant corridors and fruit houses with critical eyes. The Queen certainly had her likes and dislikes apart from bedding plants, and was not slow in showing them. She came round one day soon after I had moved over to the plant houses. We had taken a great deal of pride in growing a beautiful batch of anthuriums and had arranged it so that when she walked up one of the corridors she would be faced with this quite magnificent display, in pale pinks, whites and soft reds, all her favourite colours. She arrived accompanied by the King and other guests and (we were told afterwards, for young gardeners had to be out of the way when royals were about) took one look at the anthuriums, turned to Mr Cook and in an imperious voice said: 'Cook – have these taken away . . . terribly rude-looking things!'

Though we were not allowed to be present when Royals came visiting, from our bothy we could see them arrive. They often made a tour after church on a Sunday. I well remember one Easter Sunday seeing King George, Queen Mary, Princess Elizabeth and Princess Margaret together with several guests. And I watched the young princesses stop to pick small daffodils and give them as buttonholes to their father and to Lord Derby who was with him.

I did have one rather embarrassing experience with royalty. For some reason or other I had not been warned that Royals were coming round. I was watering in the orchard house when in walked the King and Queen. I was cornered with no way out. I was very afraid I would get into trouble for being there but I just bowed my head and kept on working and nothing was ever said.

The Royal Garden staff also had to attend to such things as the decorations in Windsor Castle during Ascot Week, and often the journeymen were sent along to help under the supervision of one of the foremen. I once went there to decorate for a banquet on Gold Cup Day. The banquet was being held in the vast Waterloo Chamber and because it was Gold Cup Day everything on the table, including the flower vases, epergnes, cutlery and so on was of gold. We gardeners were not allowed into this room, not even to take in flowers, without a butler, footman or some household official being present. The foreman did the arranging of the flowers and our job was to take the filled linings from the flower room and place them in the golden receptacles on the banqueting table. This particular foreman never carried one in himself, not because it was beneath his dignity but simply that he had usually imbibed so much drink that he was afraid of falling over and disgracing himself. He loved his beer and on these occasions being provided with an almost unlimited supply made the most of it. We would watch him swaying backwards and forwards as he arranged the flowers in the containers, almost falling over at times. Yet when he had finished, every flower would be in the right place and the arrangement would be perfect.

As the guests came into the banquet we peeped round the door and watched the King's Pipers playing them to their seats. But that was all we were allowed to see until the meal was over when we returned to collect up the flowers from the tables and bring them back into the flower room.

Another outing we looked forward to was Ascot Races to help with the decorations in the Royal Pavilion. We would be up late the previous evening cutting the roses – General MacArthur, Betty Uprichard, Hugh Dickson, Madame Butterfly and Ophelia were some of those we took – and putting them in the cool of the flower room for the night. At 5.30 next morning we loaded a van with the roses together with plenty of foliage and a selection of pot plants and without having had breakfast we were off.

At Ascot we took everything into the Royal Pavilion flower room. Then we helped whoever was in charge arrange the flowers on the tables, in the fireplaces and elsewhere. Not the outside of the Royal Pavilion, however, for this was always done by a commercial contractor. The arranging did not take long and by around 9.30 we were finished. As soon as this happened we would be given a two-gallon watering can and told to report to the butler's pantry. At the pantry the butler would take the can and, holding it under the tap of a large barrel, fill it to the top with foaming beer. The memory of that froth can make my mouth water even today. It was beautiful! The butler would also give us a

The waistcoat, apron, boots and skein of raffia were all part of a royal gardener's uniform

52

cottage loaf of bread (the one with a large base and smaller top), half a pound of butter and a huge lump of cheese. We took this back with us to the flower room and, being our first food of the day, it tasted such as I have never known bread, cheese and beer taste since.

That put us in a good mood for the rest of the day. This was our own until the races were over when we had to do the clearing up of the floral decorations. So we would watch the races, and also, between the first and second race, see the royalty coming down the course in their coaches and entering the Royal Box.

At the top of the Royal Stand was a place – it is still there – for staff. As we went through the gate at the bottom of the stand the man on duty, who knew us, would say, 'Let's have your cards,' and mark on our race-cards his forecast of the winners for the day. And, what is more, he was more often than not correct in his forecasts.

I knew little about racing. Little Horwood had been in hunting country where the only races were point-to-point at which I would perhaps have sixpence on a horse and more often lose than win. Fortunately at those point-to-points we were generally able to recoup our losses by helping to pull cars out of the mud, for it always seemed to be muddy in those days. So Ascot was my first encounter with real horseracing. The first time I went I had real beginner's luck. I had my marked card and was dutifully putting a small sum on each of the selected mounts when I happened to go out on to the stand and see a shining black horse go by. I was fascinated by it and I remember saying something like, 'By golly, that's a lovely horse; it's shining in the sun!' I decided to venture an extra sixpence on it, despite opposition from Hobday the orchid specialist who was in charge for the day, who told me severely that, 'You *never* back two horses in one race, my lad.' But it was such a lovely horse that I was determined to back my hunch. I turned to a footman who ran a book for the staff and put on my money. The horse was Lone Isle, the jockey Gordon Richards. The race started and gradually I saw Lone Isle pull away from the others, and when it went first past the winning post I nearly fell off the top of the stand in

54

excitement. It won at 100 to 6. I was rich!

Cricket was popular at Windsor and the Royal Household eleven was of a high standard: it was regarded as an honour to be picked for it. I did play a few times but I was not really good enough. Matches were played against teams from other large estates such as Mentmore, Luton Hoo and King's Waldenbury.

We also had a bowling green; but that sport was for the head gardeners and foremen only, not for us lowly improvers and journeymen.

I learnt to swim while at Windsor – in the River Thames. We used to go down to the river at the bottom of the park and I remember my pride when I managed to swim right across to the other side. I had forgotten I had to get back; but with the bothy boys encouraging me from the other bank I eventually managed it!

Christmas at Windsor was rarely a time of much celebration for those in the bothy because every gardener who could possibly do so went home for the occasion. But some – maybe three or four – had to stay and these would receive a special joint of beef from the Royal Family and Christmas pudding and mince pies from the head gardener's wife, so they did not do too badly.

Holidays of any kind were infrequent. Now and again we could put in for a long weekend – a long weekend in those days meaning Friday evening to Sunday evening – but this was only allowed, say, twice or three times a year, unless it were an emergency. So I did not get home very often and when I did go it meant getting a bus to Amersham, another to Aylesbury and yet another to Little Horwood which worked out quite expensive. I can remember a week at Castle Kennedy in Wigtonshire when we stayed with the head gardener, Bob Rye. While there we visited the gardens at Logan and other places round about which was an education for a young gardener like myself. I was amazed at the wealth of rhododendrons, azaleas, magnolias, cardiocrinums, embothriums and so on that were growing in this warm sheltered spot.

It was while I was on holiday at Castle Kennedy in 1935 that I received a telegram which was to bring a great change into my way of life.

Life in the Parks

Promotion in the Royal Gardens above journeyman-gardener was hard to come by and after over four years at Windsor, though my wages had by now risen to thirty-five shillings a week, I had decided it was time to move on. But where to go?

In the past it had been the practice for young gardeners to move from estate to estate, gathering experience (for every place had something different to offer) eventually finishing up as a head gardener. But private estates were fast on the decline as the result of taxation, higher wages, the increasing cost of materials and so forth, and we young gardeners at Windsor would often sit around in the bothy discussing what we wanted to do and wondering where the best prospects lay. In general we came to the conclusion that the future lay in the public parks. However, I did at first consider private estates and went for interviews at several including Pierpont Morgan's place near Watford. But I found nothing that suited me, and my thoughts turned more and more towards the public parks.

So I asked Bob Greenfield for his advice. Bob was the long-established representative for Peed's Seeds and I had known him from the Horwood days when he would swagger in to see Father, have a good lunch provided by Mother, and go away with a substantial order for seeds. (These seed firm men were important people in those days. The man from Suttons Seeds, for example, wore a black coat, pinstripe trousers and bowler hat and would stroll into the gardens of the big houses as if he owned them. He was always insistent that he was *not* a commercial traveller but 'a representative of the House of Sutton'. He would be given an order perhaps in the nature of £150 to £200 – a lot of money in those days – for seeds

Leeds in the days of industrial grime

56

and sundries, graciously accept a midday dinner and depart to make his leisurely way to the next aristocratic customer; arriving, if he had planned it properly, just in time for tea.) Bob Greenfield was quite a character and travelling as he did all over the country he knew what was going on in the horticultural world. He was like a father to young gardeners, giving counsel and advice. So I wrote asking if he knew of any openings for a journeyman-gardener in the parks departments. He straightaway mentioned my name to the City of Leeds Parks Department, they said they had a vacancy so he sent a telegram to me on holiday at Castle Kennedy. I went direct from there to Leeds for an interview, was successful and got the job.

Rather sadly, for it meant leaving my girl Connie, as well as many firm friends in the Royal Gardens, I left Windsor on the first day of August, 1935.

How different I found things at Leeds! It was my first experience of an industrial area and to begin with it took some getting used to. But though some of it was not very agreeable at the time, it was, in retrospect, a most valuable experience. I was sent to the gardens at Temple Newsam, quite a distance outside the city boundaries to the east. Temple Newsam House, which has been called the 'Hampton Court of the North', is a house of mellow brick filled with treasures. It is part of a large estate which formerly belonged to Lord Halifax but had been taken over by the City of Leeds whose parks department, at the time of my joining them, were engaged in the considerable operation of transforming it from a private garden into a public park.

I was in digs at Halton, a few miles outside of Leeds, with a Mrs Claughton who had been cook to Lord Irwin (later Lord Halifax) at Temple Newsam so there were no complaints about the food. She was married with one daughter. Her husband, a brassfitter, was out of work and she took in two lodgers. It was here that I was introduced to real Yorkshire pudding. The first Sunday at dinner I was given a plateful of Yorkshire pudding alone except for masses of gravy. I was told 'Those that eats most pudding gets most meat.' So I stuffed myself and found out soon after where the catch lay. The more pudding you ate the *less* meat you wanted: it was an excellent appetite satisfier.

Complete realization that I was living in the industrial North did not come to me until the first November of my stay in Leeds. I used to cycle to Temple Newsam of a morning and back at night. One day in November fog came: it fell on the place like a soft blanket, what the Leeds people called a pea-souper. Everything – buses, cars, even the trams – stopped. I don't remember how long it took me to get home that night but it was a long, exhausting, nerve-wracking time. When I eventually arrived at my lodgings and looked in a mirror I could hardly recognize myself for the patches of black under the eyes and around the nostrils. At that moment I was tempted to give up gardening for good.

But, of course, I didn't. And I am glad I refrained. For at Leeds I was able to acquire much valuable knowledge in growing under difficult industrial conditions. In those days cities did not have such clean air as they do today and in Leeds I would see tops of oak trees killed off by the sulphur in the atmosphere. At Windsor we had had to provide plants for an estate: at Leeds we had a whole city to look after with all its many activities. We did an enormous amount of bedding out from Temple Newsam but one thing always disgusted me in connection with it – the senseless waste. Every year thousands and thousands of bulbs were bought in from Holland and every year, as soon as they had flowered, they were dug out and destroyed. The head gardener insisted on total destruction and he would stand by to ensure that they were buried or put on a bonfire so that no one could possibly use them again, not even perhaps to enjoy the sight of them flowering on a waste piece of land. We did this with other things too. Azaleas, for example, were bought in by the hundred for the display houses; yet when they had finished flowering the head gardener would be there to see that they were burnt and that nobody had further use of them. That is the way things were in the public parks in those days.

In front of Temple Newsam house were extensive bedding schemes, a water garden, a kitchen garden with a high pergola in the centre, herbaceous borders

A winter scene in Derby Arboretum

around the walls and areas of grass between, on which the vegetables used to be grown. A vinery and lean-to greenhouse on the south-facing wall at the top of the kitchen garden provided a supply of ornamental and flowering plants throughout the twelve months of the year. On the walls of the lean-to greenhouse were the geraniums King of Denmark, Paul Crampel, Mme Bruant and the ivy-leaved rich pink Improved Galilee growing to a height of fifteen or more feet and flowering throughout the year. We also raised many fuchsias, hydrangeas and cyclamen much in the way I had learnt at Windsor and I found that my experience there stood me in good stead for the work in public parks.

I was in Leeds during the sad period of the death of George V. That day of January 20th, 1936 is still in my

memory, a day when the radio was informing us continually that 'the King's life is slowly drawing to a close'.

After two years at Leeds I felt I wanted a move again. So, in early 1937, I joined the Borough of Derby Parks Department. I was still a journeyman-gardener and still single, though for the past two years I had been writing every week to Connie Cook and seeing her whenever possible. Connie by now had moved to Sandringham where her father had taken the post as the royal head gardener. Things had not gone too well for C. H. Cook at Windsor after the death of George V. The new king, Edward VIII, (later Duke of Windsor) brought Mrs Simpson to Windsor Castle and some of their changes began to upset certain members of the staff. Edward VIII was no respecter of conventions and would, for example, drive his car up the Wellingtonia Walk and take a short cut to the castle through the orchard, something which did not endear him to the gardeners. On one occasion his

car got stuck in the gateway and Connie's sister Mabel went out and helped him get it free. He also began to make various economies in the gardens; one that upset C.H. (because he thought it was such a false one) was an order to cut down to pot level all the established fruit trees in the orchard house. It must have been heart breaking to see all those lovely trees go. But I understand the final straw came when Mrs Simpson walked into the greenhouse where the peaches were being grown and requested that the blossoms be cut off for her to use as decoration in the Castle.

Somehow or other, Queen Mary, now at Sandringham, heard what was going on and when her head gardener Tom Cook retired that year she invited C.H. to take over.

(C. H. Cook stayed at Sandringham until he retired in 1952 when he went to live at Dersingham, the next village to Sandringham. Queen Mary visited him here. One of his proudest possessions was a set of monogrammed cufflinks presented to him by the Queen Mother shortly after her husband's death.)

So Connie went to Sandringham. Her parents knew by now that we were writing to each other but when I paid a visit soon after they moved I received a very cool reception, especially from her mother who in no way thought a journeyman-gardener good enough for a head gardener's daughter! But this did not stop us becoming engaged soon after this.

The Derby Parks Department started me off at the Arboretum in the centre of the town; later I was moved to Darley Abbey Park on the outskirts, a private estate which, like Temple Newsam at Leeds, had been taken over and turned into a public park. The head gardener here was a man who had been in charge when Darley Abbey was a private estate. His name was John Maxfield, though, of course, we never called him by his Christian name. (It was never done in those days to address a superior so – it had to be Mister or Sir.) He was the typical old-type head gardener: he would look a man up and down and sideways to see what he was like and to ascertain if he was going to be any use to him. He judged a man in the greenhouse by the way he handled a watering can. Did he fill the pot right to the rim? Did he tap it to see if it really did need watering, or was he watering just for the sake of watering? If he had a man who used a can correctly he would do anything for him. He was perhaps the finest head gardener I ever worked under. A marvellous plantsman, he taught me, for example, more about cyclamen than I learnt elsewhere in all my life. He had cyclamen in six-inch pots eighteen or more inches across with fifty to sixty blooms to every pot. Father grew good cyclamen at Horwood House, but Maxfield grew them better. Father and he, however, had one thing in common: they both insisted that the test of a properly grown cyclamen was to take it about August or September, when it had had its final potting and just before it was ready to flower, turn it upside down and stand it on its leaves. If the leaves carried the pot, it had been correctly grown. And when John Maxfield carried out this test, and it was satisfactory, he would turn to the man who had grown it and say: 'You're not doing too bad'. Which, coming from him, was sufficient praise for those who knew and respected him.

Sandringham Parish Church

Maxfield also taught me a great deal about Gloire de Lorraine begonias. We had had these begonias, of course, at Windsor and I thought I knew everything about them. But Maxfield taught me a lot more. He produced begonias which were, without exaggeration, twenty-four inches across and the same high, with an absolute mass of flowers. I remember once staging them at a Derby Chrysanthemum Show held at the public baths in Queen Street; we put up a large group and they were a sensation.

Maxfield came round one day as I was working with begonias in a greenhouse. I was spreading soot on the staging between the pots for I had always been given to understand that the leaves of the begonias took in ammonia from the soot and that it also helped to keep down red spider. Maxfield seemed surprised: 'What are you doing that for?' he asked, and when I told him he looked at me hard and said: 'You keep down red spider by watering and spraying, and the plants feed through their roots'. But then he seemed to have second thoughts and with a, 'Well, if that's your way, carry on', went on and never mentioned it again. So I have always carried

The marriage of Percy Thrower and Constance Cook, 9th September, 1939. Left to right: Mrs Thrower, Harry Thrower (senior), Joan Thrower, Harry Thrower (junior), Percy Thrower, Connie Thrower, C. H. Cook, Mabel Cook and Mrs Cook

on this practice and, though I say it myself, I have produced many first-class Gloire de Lorraine begonias.

I had two years under John Maxfield. Sadly, in the early part of the war he died suddenly. But I value the time I spent under him: it was splendid training. He was very strict; very severe; but he taught me a heck of a lot.

The war started and with it came many changes both in my personal lifestyle and in my work. The biggest change was my getting married. Connie and I had been engaged for about a year and had arranged to get married on the second Saturday in September, 1939, provided war did not break out in the meanwhile; in which eventuality we had decided we might postpone the wedding. War was declared the Sunday before the wedding so it was panic stations. I phoned Connie at Sandringham and she was undecided. We didn't know what to do. Finally we decided to go through with it and then the fun started. Everything and everybody was disorganized for nobody knew just what was happening with regard to the war: we were expecting to be bombed, invaded, God knows what. And Sandringham being over in the east coast region nearest to Germany nobody wanted to be there.

I arrived at Sandringham on the night before the wedding and stayed with Connie's Uncle Tom. The wedding was to take place in Sandringham church but right up to practically the last minute we did not know who was coming to it. My brother Harry was to be best man but he did not think he would be able to get through from London so I got a friend, Dennis Jordan, to stand by as substitute. One of my sisters was to be bridesmaid and she and Mother and Father were to come from Little Horwood – but we had heard nothing from them.

Saturday the 9th came and it was a beautiful fine, warm day: so warm that we decided to have the reception outside the head gardener's house in the Royal Gardens. My sister and my parents arrived just in time, Father having said, I was told, 'We're going, never mind if we're bombed to pieces', and then my brother turned up to take over as best man. So all was well even though Connie

The wedding reception for over a hundred guests was held at the head gardener's house at Sandringham

was making a bouquet for my sister Joan as late as a couple of hours or so before the ceremony. Connie's sister Mabel was the other bridesmaid.

The Rev. A. R. Fuller officiated and a full choir was in attendance. Connie tells me she wore a gown of ivory satin with embroidered veil and a wreath of orange flowers. Her bouquet was of lilies and carnations. And she says the bridesmaids' dresses were of blue crêpe-de-chine with headdresses to match and their flowers were pink carnations and blue scabious. And for those who are interested in such things the organist (Mr F. J. Bone) played the Bridal March from Wagner's Lohengrin and Mendelssohn's Wedding March, while the hymns were 'Lead us Heavenly Father, lead us' and 'O Perfect Love'. About all I remember clearly is that my bride, Constance Margaret Ina, looked very lovely and that they got me to wear formal morning dress for the occasion. Over 100 guests were at the reception.

No honeymoon was possible and we returned that same evening by train to Derby where I had rented a house. We took back a cold chicken to ensure we had at least something to eat. I had the Sunday off and returned to work as usual on the Monday, for all holidays had been cancelled.

It was time of blackouts with rationing soon to come. We had practically nothing in the way of furniture or household goods but a few wedding presents helped out. Our most treasured wedding present (which we still have) was from Queen Mary – a set of Burslem china dishes together with a card personally signed by the Queen. (Though of course these were far too precious for us to use except on very special occasions.) Someone gave us a bathroom cabinet. A strange thing with me is that although I can do almost any practical job in the garden, give me a hammer and nails in the house and I'm the biggest dud in the world, as I proved with this cabinet. I put some plugs in the wall and fastened the cabinet to it carefully, but the second time I went to it the cabinet came away in my hand and I just managed to catch it before it smashed on the floor. Even worse were my experiences with an electric light bowl which the lads at the Derby Arboretum had given us. I fixed the bowl to the ceiling, put in the bulb and then left it without testing while we went out to see some friends. Coming back late that evening I switched on and nothing happened. I got a torch and was horrified to find that the bulb had fallen out of its socket and had cracked the handsome bowl underneath. I daren't tell the lads at the Arboretum but knowing they had bought it at a local electrical shop I called in and managed to buy another of the same design. Saved, I thought, though I wasn't too pleased at having to find the money for the new bowl. I put the bowl on the floor, sat myself in a low chair and began undoing the chains to put the hooks on. Then I dropped one of the hooks. And to my absolute horror it went right through the bottom of the bowl which was completely ruined for a second time. There was nothing for it but to rush back to the shop again and see if they had yet another of the same design. They had – just the one. I carried it home very, very carefully, set it up . . . and we still have it, intact, today!

However, I had been saving money (with the Leeds Permanent Building Society) and had managed to put by £124. It doesn't sound much today but it was a lot of money in those days. In fact it proved enough to furnish our house with a dining-room suite (a table, four chairs and a sideboard), a three-piece lounge suite, a bedroom suite (walnut at that!), carpets for the lounge, bedroom, stairs and spare room, a spare bed, a chest of drawers and various odds and ends, and I still had some change. That was 1939!

In 1939, too, on the last day of the year, sadly my father died, from a haemorrhage of the lungs, though I feel his death was almost as much caused by heartbreak from seeing the lovely gardens he had built up at Horwood House gradually deteriorate through lack of labour. His staff had been reduced from nineteen to three and though he tried his utmost to keep things going he fought a losing battle. When I used to go back to see him he would more than likely be in the stokehole clinkering the fire to keep it going at night and he would come out coughing and spitting from the sulphur fumes. When Father died Mother went into the House as housekeeper and when the Denny family moved from the mansion (which was

66

taken over by a girls' school evacuated from the Isle of Wight) and lived in The Laundry, a building in the village which itself was almost like a small mansion, she went with them. After Mr Denny died Mother took a cottage of her own and ran a small shop which she kept going until she was over eighty, only finishing then because she refused to adopt decimalization!

As far as work was concerned at Derby, as the war progressed many of the lads from the Parks Department either volunteered for the Forces or were called up. I was put in charge of food production and, although I volunteered twice, I was sent back each time on the grounds that I was engaged on a more important job and that I could on no account leave it. So I continued in charge of food production, growing crops at the sewage works, on spare land at the sewage farm, on the race-course, in the parks (where we also did demonstrations to show allotment holders how to get the best out of their 'Dig for Victory' plots) and in many odd places.

Any spare time I had was mostly taken up with duties as a special constable and with firewatching. And these duties were not without their perils.

Judging the corporation allotments at Derby was a job for the Parks Department. Left to right: A. J. Gathergood, John Maxfield, Percy Thrower and the Parks Superintendent, T. S. Wells

One night I was on firewatching duty at the Arboretum with as companion a young lad not long left school called Ken Hodgkinson, and we were walking through the trees of the Arboretum not far away from the greenhouses. The sirens had sounded the alert that German bombers were in the vicinity when, all of a sudden, there came a terrific explosion and not far away we saw a house literally go up in the air – its roof lifted in the blast and the walls burst asunder. Knowing by now that when one bomb fell others usually followed, I pushed Ken under a tree and went down flat myself. Lucky I did, for that instant a stick of four bombs went across the Arboretum. One hit the bandstand less than two hundred yards away; another hit one of the smoke generators that the army had installed in and around the town to put a screen of smoke over and hopefully lead the enemy bombers astray. The hit generator began to send up huge columns of smoke which made it look as if much of the town was on fire. Lying on the ground I looked over at Ken; he was where I had pushed him with his feet and head well down – but he had forgotten about his behind which was sticking right up in the air. And considering that pieces of iron (from the bandstand) had peppered the trees all around he was fortunate not to have been on the receiving end of one or he might have been prevented from sitting down for quite a while! As it was, we were both covered with dirt, rubble and dust. But I shall never forget Ken's first words to me when the bombing had passed. He said 'If this is bloomin' firewatching . . . let me stay home!' And he still maintains that I kept him busy clearing up the damage in the Arboretum for the rest of the night. Ken today is the much respected head gardener at Derby Parks.

But that was not the end of it. Someone came running to the Arboretum to inform us that, 'They've caught it bad up the London Road'. That was frightening news: that was where I lived; that was where Connie was. I grabbed my bicycle and raced off.

Demonstrating potato planting in the Old Chester Road playing fields at Derby as part of the 'Dig for Victory' campaign

The first person I saw was Connie, looking white and trembling. Thank God, she was safe. But our house! The windows were out and the ceiling down.

We made a start tidying things up and as it was winter time and cold I set about getting a fire going. We had a fireplace in the house with an oven over the top of it and in the grate I laid a fire. It was around 7.30 in the morning by then and still dark. I lit the fire and it started up well. Then I heard a roaring noise in the chimney and soon realized it was on fire. What had happened was that the oven had become clogged with soot during the bombing. We soon knew we had a chimney on fire, for lighted soot began to float down into the street below causing much consternation, for not only were we contravening the blackout regulations (as if we could help it!) but we were creating a target for any German bombers that might decide to pay another visit to our area. I quickly put it out and we had no fire in the grate that day.

A win on the pools brought this Morris 8 and the opportunity to travel

Night after night at Derby in those war years we never went upstairs but slept on a mattress under the dining room table. The Germans continually bombed neighbouring Coventry and Birmingham and we could see it all in the sky and felt very vulnerable.

Another time during the war when I got caught up in an air-raid was in 1944 when I went to London and stayed overnight with my brother. I was on my way to Wisley to take the preliminary examination of the National Diploma in Horticulture (N.D.H.). While at Leeds I had gone to horticultural classes and had also taken a postal course in horticulture. As a result of this study I managed to pass the Royal Horticultural Society's General Examination with a First-class Certificate. At Derby I had continued the postal courses and also attended Derby Technical College, eventually becoming a lecturer there. Now I was trying for my first examination of the National Diploma in Horticulture. That night in London there was an air-raid – it was the era of the buzzbomb when one heard the buzz, then quietness as the engines shut out and the bomb floated down; and finally the quietness shattered as the bomb reached its target and exploded. It was a shocking night! My brother

JF-8663

had a flat at the top of a house and we spent most of the night either under the table or under the bed. Next morning I was not exactly in the mood to face a serious examination. I took the train to Wisley, sat the exam . . . and failed hopelessly!

However, the next year I went again to Wisley and this time passed the Preliminary without much trouble. And the year after that I also passed my Final.

At the same time I was studying for the Institute of Parks Administration Diploma and had passed the Preliminary. But having obtained my N.D.H. I said to myself, 'I've got the one I want; the other doesn't matter,' and that was the end of examinations for me. I had spent so much time 'burning the midnight oil' that I just did not want any more of it.

The war years weren't easy for anyone. We continued to rent a house but I later regretted that we did not buy it instead, for we had the offer. Houses in those years were cheap and if we had taken the plunge and obtained a mortgage we could have bought it for £350 and no doubt have made a couple of thousand pounds on it when things came back to normal. But we did manage to get a small car. It came to us through the kindness of the football pools. One week Connie had filled in the coupon but had not kept a copy. It snowed that Saturday and many matches were cancelled. When I looked at the results I felt we might have won something. But I did not give it much thought and so was taken unawares when coming home for my midday meal on the Wednesday Connie said, 'The cheque's come, Percy'. It was for £52 and that bought us our first motorcar. It was a Morris Eight saloon. The man who had it for sale wanted £45 but I persuaded him to knock off a couple of pounds because it had a dud battery. That car was in use all through the war years – particularly for my police duties – with the headlamps blacked out except for a tiny slit. And it stayed with us until the end of 1947 by which time we were living at Shrewsbury. By then it had done 70,000 miles and was well past its best! I finally made up my mind to sell it after a long trip to Sandringham to see my wife's parents one Christmas. (I had the honour with Connie on this occasion of being at the royal celebrations, seeing the Christmas tree and watching the royal children receive their presents: it was a great family celebration.) On getting home I found I had developed a stiff neck and shoulders from the persistent draught through the car door. Without further ado I went to the firm of Wales and Edwards in Shrewsbury to see if they could possibly get me a new car. I was lucky and they got me a new Morris Ten. I advertised the old Morris Eight and an innkeeper on the Abbey Foregate at Shrewsbury paid me £230 10s. for it: not bad for a car that had done 70,000 miles! But that was wartime for you.

During the years at Derby I was promoted from journeyman-gardener, first to foreman then to general foreman and finally to assistant parks superintendent under T. S. Wells. When the war finished and things in England began to brighten up my thoughts turned once more to moving. I had reached as high as I could at Derby.

I applied for a position at Portsmouth. Not that I particularly wanted to go to Portsmouth but I was anxious to have the experience of being on a short list and having to attend interviews; for interviews were an important part in getting a new job in the parks departments and if one knew how to conduct oneself to advantage it was very helpful. However I did not even reach the short list at Portsmouth. A little while later, however, a parks superintendent's job at Leamington Spa came up and this time I did get on the short list. I went for my interview but lost the job by one vote; the man who got it was an old friend of mine George Ingle who had been at Leeds while I was there and since then had been in charge of Shrewsbury parks. He was a first-rate gardener so I did not feel that I had been unfairly treated. The next job to be advertised was for a superintendent for Shrewsbury Parks where my rival in the Leamington interview, George Ingle, had come from. I was put on the short list again and this time I was offered the position. I accepted and considering there had been seventy-two applicants for the job felt quite proud of myself: particularly as I became the youngest parks superintendent in the country.

The Town of Flowers

New Year's Day, 1946 – the day I took up my new appointment as parks superintendent of Shrewsbury – was cold and frosty. We motored over from Derby in the old Morris Eight, entered the lovely old town which lies within a loop of the meandering Severn and arrived at our new home – Quarry Lodge in Quarry Park.

Strange in a way that we should be coming to Shrewsbury to live for we had both been there in the past, though never together, and we had both liked the place. I had been there in the 1930s with my father for the Shrewsbury Show and Connie had gone several times also for the Show, at which her father was a judge from 1912 up until the time of his death. Mr Cook used to take his wife and two daughters Connie and Mabel with him and they had actually stayed at Quarry Lodge, the place that was now to be our home. Connie remembers being in the top bedroom of the Lodge watching the fireworks, never dreaming that one day she would be living there as the wife of a parks superintendent.

It was destined to be our home for a long time. Yet that frosty morning in 1946 when we reached Shrewsbury I recollect saying, 'I think perhaps two years here . . . and then on to something bigger.' Little did I think that thirty-one years later we would be still in Shrewsbury and not in the least wanting to leave.

The Dingle, a dell in the centre of the park with a lake and formal and informal gardens, was world renowned long before I came to Shrewsbury; in fact, it is looked upon as one of the finest pieces of bedding out in the world. However, when I took it over in 1946 it had been sadly neglected because of the war. On the other hand this did have its advantages in that I was able more or less to start from scratch. The central park had been ploughed up for vegetables; cabbage stalks, old potato tops and weeds were to be found all over the place. This area I cultivated and reseeded back to grass. A trickier problem was what to do with the ancient lime avenues of the Quarry. These trees, planted in 1719 by Thomas Wright, were mostly over a hundred feet high; one we measured after it had been felled was one hundred and thirty-three feet tall. But they had been planted too close together and being also drawn up by the light over the years were tall and slender. This wouldn't have mattered: what concerned us now was that they had become potentially dangerous because of their age; shortly before I arrived a young girl had been killed by a falling branch. Already a forestry expert had been called in and had given his opinion that the trees would have to go. And when I inspected the avenue myself I had to agree with him: the trees, most of them at any rate, had reached maturity and must come down. But the task of explaining this to the townspeople of Shrewsbury made me very unpopular for a while; they were proud of the lime avenues; and the issue even became a national one with letters to *The Times* from prominent men like Sir William Beach Thomas and Clough Williams-Ellis. I soon realized that in a town like Shrewsbury haste was made slowly – it was no use waving a big stick and trying to bring everyone round to one's own ideas: but with patience and explanation, if the matter were just, the citizens of Shrewsbury would see reason.

Before the trees were felled, however, an abundance of outside expert advice was both sought and given. There were those, and many of them, who felt that just topping would be sufficient. But I argued that the trees had reached too great an age for that to have much effect. It was far better, I maintained, to sweep them out completely and replant. And, eventually, this is what I did, avenue by avenue. We cut round the trees so that roots and tops came out together rather than cutting the tops and then having the arduous job of digging the out the roots separately. And when they were felled we found that most of the trees were hollow: mistletoe had worked its way into many of them, bees had made their home in some and wasps in others. Slowly we cleared the avenues and replanted – not until 1952 was the last tree cut down.

Today when I look at those avenues with the trees set farther back from the road and spaced out, I am sure I did the right thing. And I believe the people of Shrewsbury, when they saw the young avenues taking shape, forgave me for what I had done.

February that first year saw the worst flooding that Shrewsbury had experienced for sixty-five years. The army and the navy had to be brought in to rescue marooned inhabitants when the Severn overflowed its banks. At one time Kingsland toll bridge was the only road link with the outside world.

On the Dingle pond we had a flat-bottomed boat which we used when cleaning out the pond or going over to the various small islands. At two o'clock one morning there came a bang on our door. It was the Highways Department wanting to borrow this boat. 'The river's in flood,' they said, 'it's out in the streets'. Alarmed, I said, 'My car's at the highway depot in Smithfield Road down by the river.' But they assured me that the river had never been known to flood as high as that. But it did. When it grew light that morning I looked out and the river water was right across the bottom of the Quarry, out on the streets and I couldn't even get to the depot where my car was – it was under four feet of water. The river that day rose nineteen feet six inches above the normal level. I was made a flood warden and took our flat-bottomed boat around the flooded streets of Shrewsbury serving hot meals to people through their bedroom windows. Another warden used an ancient coracle to take drinking water to people. It was possible to row a boat up the aisle of the Abbey church, buses and cars ran only to the outskirts of the town and there were raised platforms for people to walk on.

The following year it flooded again, not quite as bad, but over eighteen feet. We were more prepared this time and went around early helping people to get their furniture out. Many of the houses we visited still had the marks of the previous year's water and a strong fusty smell.

As in the rest of the country fuel restrictions were

enforced in Shrewsbury and we were only allowed to use it for heating greenhouses if seventy-five per cent. of their area was producing food. But I did the best I could to build up flower stocks for the future. In one of the houses were fifty oldish fuchsia plants – Mrs Marshall, Brutus, Marinka, Lena and Ballet Girl – as well as a number of begonia tubers. I started in the January with the fuchsias taking the young tips and as soon as these were rooted taking new tips. Then I went over them and took the side shoots. By the end of May when bedding out time came I had over five thousand fuchsias; which is one reason, I suppose, why fuchsias since that time have been so popular in Shrewsbury. We have used them in the beds, grown standards, had borders of more than a hundred different varieties and put them all over the place in hanging baskets. The begonias I started off early, cut them up into pieces and finished up with four times the number with which I had started.

As a novelty I grew bananas. At Derby, in Darley Abbey Park, there had been a stove house in which was a fruiting banana: when I came to Shrewsbury I brought a sucker of the plant with me and fruited bananas in the warm house.

One thing I had better mention here before I forget it. That is women gardeners. For some reason or other a few people have the impression that I am against women gardeners. That isn't so. Women gardeners were looked down on in the days of private service – they weren't considered good enough for such a skilled job! But war changed all that. They were employed at Windsor in the 1914–18 war and in the 1939–45 war in the parks at Derby they did a first-class job. When I arrived at Shrewsbury there were two women on the staff.

Another decision taken the first year was to to make Shrewsbury a 'Town of Flowers' with a floral display throughout the whole of the summer season, not just during the two days of the Floral Fête. This Floral Fête, or to give it its more official title, the Shrewsbury Flower Show, had been a casualty of the war years but was due to open again in 1947. I helped to devise a scheme whereby business houses, including the hotels, competed in floral display. The *Shrewsbury Chronicle*

Shrewsbury Flower Show in the late 1940s

put up a silver cup for the best decorated premises with a frontage of over forty feet, the Chamber of Commerce gave a similar cup for premises under this size while the Licensed Victuallers Association awarded one for the best decorated licensed premises. We in the Parks Department helped with plants and advice and I got Connie's father, C. H. Cook, and another famous gardener, A. E. Fox, from Hope Court, Ludlow, to act as judges the first year. We also put floral arrangements wherever we could – on traffic islands for example and on the fronts of public buildings. It proved a great success, with over a hundred business establishments entering the competition, and it made the reputation of Shrewsbury as a 'Town of Flowers' which it has maintained ever since.

In a way it was this competition in 1946 for a floral Shrewsbury that started me off in broadcasting. At that time the BBC were doing a radio programme called *Round and About* and David Martin who ran it interviewed the two judges of the competition and myself in Shrewsbury's Lion Hotel in Wyle Cop. The interview was done on a disc (not on tape as it is today) and afterwards we had the disc played back to us, the first time I had ever heard my own voice recorded.

The Shrewsbury Flower Show duly returned the following year. The sixtieth held by the Shropshire Horticultural Society over a period of seventy-three years, it was held, as before, in the Quarry. It proved more popular than ever. We had 120,000 visitors in the two days with takings of £40,000 as compared with the £790 at the first show in 1875 and £13,000 in 1939, the last time it had been held. But it was a hot show – do you remember that summer of 1947? – and though the seeding down to grass of the Quarry had taken well the turf was not established enough to withstand such an influx of people. Queues were everywhere – for food (still in short supply), for beer, even to get into the large marquees – and I can even now see in my mind's eye the dust rising like a cloud over the whole Quarry. At the end of the first day all the exhibits, roses, dahlias, chrysanthemums, fruit and vegetables, were covered in a film of grey dust. Our house in the Quarry did not escape; a film of dust settled over mantelpieces, furniture, everywhere. But that was only a minor irritant; the Show itself was a great success.

In 1947 I was appointed honorary adviser to the Shropshire Horticultural Society, a position I held until 1975 when I was appointed chairman – a great honour – for the Society, which celebrated its centenary in 1974, is one of the largest and richest in the world. In 1948 a separate parks department for Shrewsbury was formed and I was made Chief Officer. Before that the department, like those in many other boroughs, had been under the control of the Borough Surveyor. I was now more or less my own boss.

A small item which also comes to mind from 1948 is that at the Show in the August I exhibited 'a light-blue flower, the size of a shilling, with dark foliage' which aroused quite a lot of interest especially from women visitors. The *Daily Mail* reported the story under the headline 'Flower with Strange Lure for Women' and quoted me as saying that its attraction for women was 'most strange' as it had no smell and the flower was small. The parent plant came from the Royal Gardens at Sandringham and I had two varieties of it – the other had dark blue flowers. It was, in fact, none other than the saintpaulia, the African violet, now a common house plant but then a rarity.

One day that autumn I was busy in my office in the Quarry when a man walked in and said, 'You don't know me, but the name is Godfrey Baseley. I'm from the BBC.'

'Oh, yes,' I said, 'and what can I do for you?'

'I've just been down what you call the Dingle, into the garden,' he said, 'who's responsible for that?'

I admitted responsibility and he went on: 'I do a radio programme every Sunday afternoon called *Beyond the Back Door*. It's a bit of "Dig for Victory", something on flowers, backyard poultry, rabbits and so on. Enough to make up a half-hour programme with about ten minutes devoted to gardening. Would you like to join me on it?'

Not really knowing what I was letting myself in for I said yes, and arranged to meet him and Leonard Clift in the Quarry the following Sunday to talk about making a small shrubbery. I collected together a few small shrubs ready to plant in a border near to one of the greenhouses. By the time Sunday came I was so nervous that I could eat no breakfast or lunch. However, it turned out not to be too bad and when the programme was over Godfrey said, 'It's a live programme. I've had your voice recorded in Birmingham; if it comes over all right, how would you like to come along to the studio on the first Sunday in every month and talk about the month's work in the garden?'

I replied to the effect that I would try anything once.

Godfrey telephoned a few days later. 'I've heard that recording. It's first class. Now I want you to prepare a script to run for about ten minutes, on the work to do in the garden during the coming month'.

I prepared a script, read it through to myself, timed it and sent it off. Godfrey rang again: 'Yes . . . ideal'.

On the Sunday I went along to the studio in Birmingham. I had never been in a studio before in my life and I wasn't comfortable sitting at the table. Tony Shryane was the studio manager (Tony continues today as the editor and producer of *The Archers*) so I said to him, 'Can I stand up? I'm not comfortable sitting down.' Tony gave me a look. 'Nobody ever stands up in a studio to do a recording,' he said severely. But I insisted that I would feel much more at ease if I stood up, and so he had a music stand brought in on which he placed the small desk that held my script (to prevent a hollow sound) and told me to stand up and get on with it. I was so nervous that I had to keep my knees together to stop them knocking. But I managed to read my script without too much trouble – and that was the beginning of what was to be a long career in broadcasting – carried out whenever possible standing up!

Each first Sunday in the month I continued with this programme and then every third Sunday I began to visit somebody's garden and talk about it over the air. We went to Shipton-on-Stour to see a sweet pea grower; to Hope Court, Ludlow, for an interview with that wise old gardener A. E. Fox; to Weston-under-Lizard, the Earl of Bradford's place, for another good gardener Roland Smith; to the outskirts of Wednesbury where someone was gardening successfully on boulder clay and slag heaps; and others. We returned a second time to Hope Court, Ludlow and this time met the owner, Mrs Leese, a very keen gardener. In conversation she asked Godfrey Baseley what he called his programme and on receiving the reply, '*Beyond the Back Door*, Madam,' she looked at him rather straight and said, 'But surely *my* garden is not a "beyond the back door" one?' And that I believe is why the name of the programme was soon afterwards changed to *In Your Garden* under which name it was to prove so popular to Sunday afternoon listeners. And it went on until television started in 1951.

One would think that politics could never come into a gardening programme, but just before the 1951 general election I was asked to refrain from recommending a Michaelmas daisy called Winston Churchill as 'the best red' – it was classed as a political reference. I had to supply the name the following week when the election was over!

The next big event in Shrewsbury was the Royal Show in 1949. Attended by Princess Elizabeth, the Duke of Edinburgh and other royal personages it attracted vast crowds and certainly gave the parks department plenty to do. We supplied some 150,000 flowering plants for what was generally acknowledged to be the best floral display the Royal had ever had. At the ornamental garden in front of the entrance to the show ground more than 2,500 pink geraniums and purple heliotropes were interspersed with salvias and bordered with blue lobelia. Another quite dazzling display was provided in front of the Royal Pavilion. We got through over 80,000 flower pots and laid some thirty acres of turf. For the two months previous to the opening, my men worked on average from 7.00 in the morning till 11.00 at night. It was the biggest job I had ever directed. On the Sunday I broadcast my *In Your Garden* programme from the Royal Show grounds.

In February, 1950, I began a monthly ten-minute gardening talk, *Our Garden* in the BBC Midland Region Children's Hour using at first the flower plots in the Quarry to illustrate the talks. Produced by Peggy Bacon, the aim of the programme was to encourage children in gardening and to help stop vandalism in the parks. Four local boys

An early broadcast with Roland Smith from the gardens of the Earl of Bradford at Weston-under-Lizard

and four local girls began cultivating a special border in the Quarry. We then contacted the main towns in the Midlands: Birmingham, Leicester, Nottingham, Derby, Northampton, Gloucester, Hereford, Wolverhampton and Coventry – even Norwich and Great Yarmouth for they were in the Midland Region then – and asked them, too, to provide a Children's Hour garden in their public parks. It was mostly hardy annuals; sowing, thinning and the like. I would visit the parks and do a ten- to fifteen-minute programme with the parks superintendent or whoever was in charge and with the children

who were actually looking after the garden. In the September of the following year an *Our Garden* Flower Show was held when selected children from the Midland Region took their plants and flowers to the BBC studios at Birmingham to compete for prizes, the judges being Roland Smith and myself. At the 1952 *Our Garden* show two of my daughters, Margaret, then eight, and Susan, only three, took part: Susan was the youngest competitor in the show but Margaret had been taking part ever since it started. Reporting this, one of the local papers advised me to 'look to my laurels' as regards Margaret. Ann, my youngest daughter, also took part later.

The last Children's Hour Show was televised and Godfrey Baseley and myself jointly gave a cup while the BBC added another so there was one for children up to ten

Our Garden was first broadcast by BBC (Midland) Children's Hour in 1950

and another for the ten- to fifteen-year-olds. When the Children's Hour programmes finished the BBC had the cups but when we started up the classes for children in the Shrewsbury Flower Show the BBC gave them to us and they are still awarded every year in these classes.

Going back to my daughters for a moment, the local paper wasn't far wrong as regards Margaret. She went on from there to give demonstrations of flower arranging, to lecture in many parts of the country and to win prizes at the Shrewsbury Show and elsewhere. I gave her what encouragement I could but I never pushed her into horticulture. Then she decided to take up teaching and went to a training college. Her first job on leaving was at Ludlow where she taught rural science which included a good deal of gardening. In charge of the school gardens she had a greenhouse and experimental plots to look after. She stayed at Ludlow for six years. In the meantime I had bought the nursery business of Murrells at Shrewsbury and was running it in partnership with Duncan

Murphy and Margaret would give a hand at weekends. She liked the work and finally decided to give up teaching and come in with me full time. She continued with her demonstrations and lectures and soon began to appear in television programmes.

Ann, now married, has a garden of her own and is a little more keen than she used to be. But Susan, despite her *Our Garden* experience, will agree with me, I know, when I say she 'doesn't know a daisy from a dandelion'.

July 1952 brought me my first trip out of England when I went to Germany on behalf of the Shropshire Horticultural Society to plan an English garden in Berlin. The idea came from Major General G. K. Bourne, G.O.C. the British Sector in Berlin, who wrote to E. P. Everest the chairman of the Shropshire Horticultural Society, (Everest's son, a wing-commander in the RAF, was with Bourne in Berlin), asking if the Society would assist in a project for laying out, and obtaining plants and seeds for, a garden which was to be a gesture of kindness to the Berlin people. The Society agreed and Everest said to me: 'I want you to go over and meet the parks superintendent of Berlin and plan an English garden sponsored by our Society.'

So I went to Berlin. It was the first time I had flown anywhere and I was not particularly looking forward to it. We went from Northolt aerodrome and even before I got on the plane I was scared. We set off in a thunderstorm and sitting by a window I could see a tiny nut bobbing up and down on the wing outside. I don't think I took my eye off that nut all the way to Germany!

Herr F. Witte the parks superintendent met me. I was relieved to find he spoke quite good English and, in fact, we got on exceptionally well. He was a good gardener and knew his stuff. He took me out into the Tiergarten not far from the Brandenburg Gate. The whole area had been badly bombed and the Tiergarten itself, which covers some eight hundred acres and is regarded by the Berliners much as Londoners regard Hyde Park, was

At Shrewsbury Flower Show with (from left to right) Eric Robinson, Harry Wheatcroft and Geoff Grier of Wilkinson's Sword

84

practically denuded of trees – they had been cut down to provide fuel during the Russian blockade in the terrible winter of 1948. The site we chose was littered with rubble and the few large trees that remained were shattered and blasted. The site also included the ruins of a villa.

We pegged out an area of about six acres, rough-sketched a plan on paper and went back to Witte's office where his staff got busy and produced a proper plan drawn to scale. I returned to England with the plan and the Shropshire Horticultural Society approved it.

The flight back, by the way, was as bad as the one out. It was a different aircraft this time and it looked even worse than the one I had gone out in as was borne out by the stewardess who informed me, 'This one won't be as comfortable . . . but there's a strike on at Northolt and we have to use this old Dakota.' I thought of all the stories I had heard about Dakotas crashing and had a miserable flight.

At the next Shrewsbury Flower Show we went round our exhibitors, told them what we were doing and asked for their support. The President of the Society, Lieutenant General Sir Oliver Leese, was a friend of Major General Bourne in Berlin and added his support to the appeal. Photographs and plans of the suggested garden were displayed in the main marquee with an invitation to subscribe gifts of plants, trees and so forth. Soon the gifts began to roll in and we collected them together at Shrewsbury. Among them were roses from Gregory and Wheatcroft, herbaceous plants from Bakers and Bees, shrubs from Treasures of Tenbury, liliums and bulbs from Wallace and Barr, grass seed from Suttons and Carters, and much else besides. We wrote to the Queen asking if she would help and back came a letter to say that she would make arrangements for us to have plants from the Savill Gardens at Windsor. So Everest and myself went to Windsor where Sir Eric Savill took us round the lovely gardens he had developed since 1936 (with the approval of the King and Queen) and which was mainly devoted to naturalistic planting with just the kind of plants we were looking for. Sir Eric selected rhododendrons, shrubs, dahlias, hydrangeas, primulas, astilbes, many waterside plants, a metasequoia (then quite rare) – a full collection in fact – and they all came to Shrewsbury where, with the others, they were packed up and sent out to Berlin.

In the meantime I had sent Witte pictures of gardens in England showing in particular drifts of daffodils and snowdrops beneath trees and groupings of plants by the waterside. Witte had an excellent ability for landscaping and for copying and he succeeded in making a fine garden. From the photographs he sent back it was typically English, an oasis of peace and beauty. Waste swampy land was excavated to form a lake while the soil from the excavation was used to make a rock garden and shrub and flower borders. Bordering the lake were many moisture-loving plants, especially the candelabra primulas and *Primula sikkimensis*. Winding paved paths were flanked by borders of rhododendrons, azaleas, ericas and a collection of ornamental trees and shrubs with bluebells, daffodils and other bulbs naturalized among them. Witte was particularly proud of his English style lawns with close-cut, weed-free turf, which was a good advertisement for the seed sent out by English firms.

Later Witte came over for the Shrewsbury Show and stayed with us for three weeks. We were able to take him round many English gardens which he thoroughly enjoyed, and when he returned to Germany he was able to incorporate into the Berlin garden many of the things he had seen.

The garden was officially opened in June 1952 by Anthony Eden the Foreign Secretary.

Witte's daughter also came and stayed with us for about two months to learn English and she and my daughters got on very well. She must have been about sixteen at the time. An aftermath of this: when I appeared in the television programme *This Is Your Life* last year the Berlin garden was mentioned and into the studio came a very attractive woman bearing a branch of the yellow *Hamamelis mollis*. It was Herr Witte's daughter. (Witte himself died a few years ago.) I asked her if she remembered the name of the shrub she was carrying. 'Of course I do,' she replied, 'I *am* a gardener's daughter.'

Britain's Head Gardener

Television more or less began for me as a result of the making of the English garden in Berlin. Godfrey Baseley and I were invited to Vestry Hall in Birmingham to appear on Joan Gilbert's BBC Television programme, *Picture Page*, to show plans of the garden, to explain why it was being done and how it was being sponsored by the Shropshire Horticultural Society.

Soon after this a programme called *Country Calendar* started with Godfrey Baseley as editor and Barrie Edgar as producer. To begin with it came from the grounds of the Staffordshire Farm Institute (now Staffordshire College of Agriculture) at Penkridge and included a little of almost everything to do with the countryside – shooting, walking, cycling, birdwatching, angling, crafts such as thatching, wheelwrighting, blacksmithing and, of course, gardening. I did the gardening spot – and it was done outside, in all kinds of weather. After Penkridge we went to Kettering, then to Maxstoke a farm between Birmingham and Coventry where the farmer's garden was adapted with a wide concrete path down the centre to take the cameras; a greenhouse was erected and various vegetables and flowers planted. Roland Smith of Weston Park used to join me and we did a regular ten- to fifteen-minute programme. From this it went to *Out and About* on Sunday afternoons when the programmers went out to do the cycling, the angling, the birdwatching and so on. Sir Stephen Tallents was in the studio in Lime Grove as link man. When that finished it became *Club Night* with its Smokers' Club, Inventors' Club, Asiatic Club and Gardening Club. *Gardening Club* went on the air once a month. The other Clubs gradually fell by the wayside but Gardening went from strength to strength, first to once a fortnight and then to a regular spot once a week.

Gardening Club continued right up until colour television started. Gardening is a subject that cries out for colour for it really brings such a programme to life. So with the advent of colour television gardening was given more prominence. It became *Gardeners' World* which we started in the BBC garden adjoining the Botanic Garden in Birmingham. The producer, Paul Morby, first took over one allotment then gradually extended it to six, though I kept saying to him, 'It's all right for you . . . but all this has to be maintained.' I don't think he realized just what it takes to look after six standard allotments, each measuring thirty yards by ten yards. 'Oh, we can manage it,' he assured me; but before long we were in such a mess that the BBC were getting complaints from visitors who found the allotments a mass of weeds. After a while I could take no more so I wrote a letter to the BBC and that was the end of the Birmingham garden for me.

A *Gardening Club* broadcast from Gosta Green in 1957

In due time Paul Morby left the BBC and for the next two or three programmes of *Gardeners' World* various professionals were brought in to do the interviewing, the arranging and the organizing. Barry Bucknell, the do-it-yourself man, was asked to build a gazebo which, it was rumoured, cost the BBC £3000! Then I was asked back to work under Bill Duncalf who had been with me before on a programme about grass from the Surbiton grass tennis courts in the early days when we had been doing *Out and About* on Sunday afternoons, one of the few programmes broadcast from outside. Since then he had been abroad but now he came back and took over as producer of *Gardeners' World*.

Producers have played an important part in my television career and I have made many good friends among them. Barrie Edgar was my first – for the interview I did on the Berlin Garden for *Picture Page* in 1951. The first I had in London was David Attenborough who later became head of BBC2. Then came Kenneth Milne-Buckley whose wife was Sylvia Peters and after him John Furness. When we moved to Birmingham John Farringdon took over and then the job went to his floor manager Paul Morby. When *Gardeners' World* came along it was Bill Duncalf until 1972 when, strange enough, Barrie Edgar took over – a reunion after so many years – and we continued together right up to the time of my leaving the BBC in 1976.

I am often asked what goes on when a gardening programme is made for television. I have done it so many times that it all seems quite simple to me and I forget that it is a strange world to others. It is certainly a fascinating procedure.

Many people think that programmes such as those from The Magnolias are 'live' – that is, they go out direct to viewers. But of course they do not. For one thing, at nine o'clock at night (which was when *Gardeners' World* came to the screen) there is not much light left in a garden whatever time of the year it is; and a garden lit by studio lights would give horrible results, I should think. So these programmes are recorded. *Gardeners' World* was recorded once a fortnight, usually on a Tuesday, and two editions were filmed on the same day,

The studio floor at Gosta Green during a broadcast of *Gardening Club*

one in the morning which viewers saw on Friday of the same week and the other in the afternoon which was shown a week later.

The recording is generally done on magnetic or Video tape which is the same sort of tape as is used for cassette sound recording but is much wider. As with sound the tape looks exactly the same after the recording has been made as it did before. But tape has the great advantage over film in that it can be played back instantly so that one can check if a sequence has been recorded satisfactorily or not. In the old days of film we had to wait until the negative had been processed before we were able to see a print. And also in those days the sound would have been recorded separately with the result that it took many days in the cutting room before the edited film was produced. Nowadays at the end of a recording session of *Gardeners' World* the producer goes off with two fully edited and complete programmes ready for immediate transmission.

But tape has some disadvantages. For example, in the old film days all that was needed to do a recording was one film camera with its crew of four or five. Today, to record a tape, a full-size Outside Broadcast Unit is brought in with heavy electronic cameras. This necessitates at least four large and heavy vehicles from one of which, the mobile control room, cables are connected to the four large colour cameras mounted on 'dollies' or travelling carriages.

As a consequence small gardens are out for this kind of recording. This is why most of the *Gardeners' World* programmes came from places like The Magnolias or Clacks Farm, both of which have been specially adapted for this kind of work. The vehicles also need hard standing on which to park at around one thousand feet from whatever part of the garden is being dealt with. Then the cables have to be laid to the cameras. You should see The Magnolias garden when about thirty technicians and riggers are busy at work!

The producer sits in the mobile control room faced by a gallery of television sets; on his right is the sound department and on his left are the engineers who control the electronic equipment which shows the producer just what each camera is seeing in its lenses. The producer can talk to the cameramen through a microphone and headphones; he can select the pictures he wants and pass them on to the mobile videotape recording vehicle accompanied by the monitored sound.

I never prepare a script for my programmes. My method is to talk naturally about the subject agreed on and leave it to the producer to find the right pictures.

The Magnolias is not an easy place for television for it is on a sloping site and the cameras have to be propped up to get them level. And as the televising has to be done mostly out of doors the weather is very important – but unfortunately there is no picking and choosing the weather conditions.

One has to be prepared for all sorts of emergencies when broadcasting. Once I was with Arthur Billitt at

Barry Bucknell joined the programme on various occasions to give advice on constructional matters

Gosta Green and we were about to begin a programme when we saw smoke coming out of the producer's box. Within seconds all the lights went out. I shouted 'Follow me' to Arthur and we were out of that place in a hurry, I assure you. But it was only a blown fuse and we were soon back recording again. I recall another little incident which I don't suppose any viewer ever noticed. We had a real greenhouse filled with plants in the grounds of Gosta Green but in the studio we substituted a dummy one with a hinged frame and no glass. Plants were brought in and placed in this for the programme. But we had to pretend it was a real greenhouse and on one occasion wanting to open the door and finding it sticking a little, without thinking I put my hand through where the glass should be and opened the door from the inside!

On another occasion we had been warned that there would probably be an interruption during the gardening programme for a special announcement – the engagement of Princess Margaret. It duly came at a moment when I was showing viewers how to plant a gooseberry bush. So when we came back on the air I said something about all of us wanting to congratulate the Princess on her engagement and wish her every happiness. But I rather spoiled it, I think, by adding, 'And now back to the gooseberries.'

My only experience to date of doing a television programme abroad has been from the Floralies horticultural show in Paris. I had to use the facilities of French television which are rather different from ours here. In addition the building was a new one and with thousands and thousands of people having walked on the concrete floor a film of white dust had settled over everything. The woman announcer had gone for a hair-do and had not only been late getting back but had arrived without her contact lenses. As I waited for the signal to begin from the floor manager I could see her struggling to read her script – she couldn't even see the monitor! – while the cameraman seemed to be asleep with his head on his arms. But on the signal the announcer managed to say more or less the right things, the cameraman sprang into action, swinging his camera at me almost without warning, and I was able to present quite an interesting programme mainly on the fine RHS exhibit from Wisley Gardens and a collection of British orchids.

The BBC staff like to play practical jokes at times. At Birmingham when I was doing a regular live thirty-minute show I would arrive for rehearsals in the morning and before starting always hang my coat on a hook behind the greenhouse door. This was my sort of trade mark. On one occasion, however, I made three attempts to hang it up and each time it slid off on to the floor. A rubber hook had been substituted for the real one!

One of my oldest friends in the broadcasting business is Arthur Billitt. We have been friends since before the war at Derby when I was swotting up for my RHS General Examination and the National Diploma of

At Clacks Farm with Arthur Billitt and Whisky

Barrie Edgar, the producer of many editions of *Gardeners' World*, with the author on the occasion of his 1,000th television appearance

Horticulture and I used to go over to Lenton where Arthur was in charge of the Boots trial grounds and there was able to pick up much valuable information. During the war we got together on lecturing and demonstrating model allotments, and this was followed by 'Dig for Victory' with Arthur and I on the panel with C. H. Middleton. (Back in the bothy days at Windsor I had listened to C. H. Middleton never dreaming that the time would come when I would be broadcasting with him, let alone on my own.)

The BBC went to the Lenton research station for some of its early gardening programmes and when television started Arthur came up to the studios in London, then into the gardens at Birmingham and when he acquired Clacks Farm at Ombersley near Droitwich in Worcestershire the link with him became even closer. He bought Clacks Farm, not because of the house, but because of the soil which is some of the finest I have ever seen. You feel you could almost eat it – and certainly the plants appreciate it. If every soil was like that, gardening would be always easy.

Arthur found Clacks Farm in 1956. He tells the story of how he was staying in Worcestershire to take part in two 'Brains Trusts' for fruit growers at Ledbury and Evesham and looking through some estate agents' brochures came across 'Clacks Farm, Boreley, Ombersley, 36 acres', for sale. He found the place covered with seedling trees, brambles and weeds with here and there in the undergrowth discarded farm equipment. But a test with a spade showed that the soil was good – light to medium loam overlying old red sandstone. It took him five years, working weekends mostly, to clear the site.

Arthur and I *are* friends. I say that again for the benefit of a few people who think that because we have a dig at each other on programmes we are not.

During the time we were doing *Gardening Club* I took part in a number of *Woman's Hour* programmes where well-known personalities, particularly Frank Muir and Isobel Barnett, appeared with me. For one of the programmes I went to the garden of Eric Robinson and his wife Nicky. We filmed a piece on his roses, for he was a keen rose grower. We became great friends and stayed so until his unfortunate death. His stepdaughter married David Nixon who has become another good friend of ours.

Then the children's programme *Blue Peter* started a garden at the back of the Wood Lane Television Centre at Shepherd's Bush. The plot was only twelve feet by ten feet but it was amazing what we managed to produce from it – beans, peas, carrots, onions, radish, parsley and quite a few flowers as well. The garden became a popular part of *Blue Peter* and I was glad to take part in it for I always like to encourage children in gardening. Not only is it a healthy out-of-doors occupation, but these young gardeners are the customers of the future for the horticultural industry. That is one reason we keep the children's classes going at the Shrewsbury Flower Show: we must cater for the youngsters and

With Eric and Ernie in *The Morecambe and Wise Show* in 1971

encourage them, for they are our future exhibitors. The *Blue Peter* garden created an immense amount of interest and brought in an enormous amount of correspondence.

I also took part in one or two rather different kinds of programmes. I was with Benny Hill twice and was able to appreciate the work that great comedian puts into his programme. I was also a guest on the Morecambe and Wise Show. These appearances were different inasmuch as I had to work from a script, something I never do in my gardening talks. I had to remember my lines so as to give the others their lead. But they were fine people to work with and highly amusing too.

PERCY THROWER

itched!
The Beeb throw out Thrower

By KENELM JENOUR

TELEVISION gardener Percy Thrower has been sacked after nearly thirty years with the BBC — because he has recorded commercials for ITV.

Percy, 63, who presents Gardener's World on BBC-2, recorded his final programme this week for screening next Wednesday.

Since he began with the Beeb in 1947, Percy has been heard more than 700 times on BBC statemen...

Percy Thrower contract with BBC ended

By a Staff Reporter

Mr Percy Thrower's connexion with the BBC which has lasted for 29 years was severed yesterday because he is to appear in advertisements for gardening products on commercial television. He recorded his last edition of *Gardeners' World* earlier this week, screening on March 31.

Mr Philip Sidey, head of C's network programme centre in Birmingham said yesterday: "I am sorry... e to this parting of... it is inevitable.... ed as good fri... d: "It is not... ave sacked hi... over vention of the b... he seen giv...

PERCY THROWER PRUNED BY BBC OVER TV ADVERTS

By RICHARD LAST, Television Staff

...ER Britain's best known ... dropped by BBC ... years as a broadcaster signed for a series of ...er channel.

...ast appearance in his own "Gardeners' World," next he will be seen in most ITV areas advertising gardening products for ICI.

"The BBC sai...

Percy Thrower finds himself in the fertiliser

PERCY THROW

Mr Greenfingers pruned by BBC

BRITAIN'S head gardener Percy Thrower has been pruned by the BBC.

After nearly thirty years of broadcasting he has been sacked—.

By DAVID R

...for making commercials fertilizer.

Percy, 62, in his Garden TV series

I stayed with *Gardeners' World* until the early part of 1976 when, through a disagreement over my advertising of products on Independent Television, the BBC dropped me from the programme. I went ahead with commercial advertising and then Southern Television asked me to do a series of programmes on 'Great Gardens of the South' which were screened in early 1977. I enjoyed this series for it took me to many gardens I had not seen before. We started at the Royal Horticultural Society's Garden at Wisley and then went to twelve others of which Longford Water Garden (the finest I have seen of this kind anywhere) and Mottisfont Abbey (with its famous trees including the largest plane tree in Britain) were perhaps outstanding. I have also been doing a weekly radio piece (on Saturdays and Sundays) for London Broadcasting (LBC) who network it throughout most of the local stations.

Writing started as a result of television. I was doing *Gardening Club* at Lime Grove studios one day when Arthur Hellyer and Peter Ayres, editor and photograper respectively of *Amateur Gardening*, came along to watch a programme being made. When it was over Arthur Hellyer said to me, 'Would you like to write for *Amateur Gardening*?' So I began writing weekly notes for the magazine and have now been doing it for over twenty years.

The first local paper I contributed to was the *Express and Star* at Wolverhampton. They paid me five pounds a time if I remember rightly.

I wrote for the *Kidderminster Shuttle*, the *Shropshire Magazine*, the *ICI Magazine*, *Radio Times* (for five years) and many others including that famous old magazine *John Bull*. I remember this magazine especially because, after I had been writing for it for some time, they asked me to do a combined article with Richard Dimbleby. I was flattered for Richard Dimbleby had been a favourite of mine for many years and I always considered that for big occasions such as the Coronation he was unbeatable. He took me to his mother's garden where photographs were taken and we talked about lawns, dahlias and general things in the garden, and it duly appeared as an article.

The first national newspaper I contributed to was *Empire News*, which was taken over by the *Sunday Dispatch*, in turn taken over by the *Sunday Express*. I stayed with the *Sunday Express* a number of years then one day I was asked up to Fleet Street to meet the editor. Almost his first words to me were, 'Well, of course, your articles are all right . . . but some of them read a bit puddingy.' I asked him what he meant exactly. 'Not enough life in them,' was his reply. It was obvious we approached the subject from entirely different viewpoints so I finished with the *Sunday Express*.

Soon afterwards I received a letter from the *Daily Express* in Manchester and as a result of this I wrote for a number of years for northern gardeners in the Manchester edition of the paper.

It seemed that no sooner was one outlet gone than another appeared. This time it was the *Daily Mail* with an invitation to come to London to discuss a weekly piece. They told me that they wanted to make the *Daily Mail* gardening page the best in the national press and would like me to do it. I began my weekly contribution and have been writing for them ever since.

After about three years of writing weekly gardening notes for *Amateur Gardening* Arthur Hellyer said to me one day, 'Well, now, Percy, what about a book?' So I wrote my first book and it came out as *In the Flower Garden with Percy Thrower*, published by Collingridge in 1957. *In Your Garden with Percy Thrower* followed in 1959, (this being extensively revised and re-presented in 1973). This was followed by *Percy Thrower's Picture Book of Gardening* in 1961. Since then I have written:

Percy Thrower's Encyclopedia of Gardening, 1962
In Your Greenhouse with Percy Thrower, 1963 (revised in 1972)
Percy Thrower's Practical Guides, 1964 to 1968
Percy Thrower's Guide to Colour in Your Garden, 1966 (completely revised and re-presented in 1976)
Percy Thrower's Garden Notebook, 1966
Percy Thrower's Everyday Gardening in Colour, 1969
Percy Thrower's Gardening Year, 1973
Percy Thrower's Guide to Gardeners' World, 1973
Fresh Vegetables and Herbs from Your Garden, 1974

Summer-flowering plants on the patio bring colour right up to the windows of the author's home

Opposite
The rock garden and poolside
at The Magnolias in summer

Percy Thrower's Practical Guide to Roses, 1974
Percy Thrower's Step by Step Gardening, 1974
Gardening Is Fun with Percy Thrower, 1976
Percy Thrower's How to Grow Vegetables and Fruit, 1977
To begin with the books were published by W. H. & L. Collingridge Limited until, in 1967, this firm was incorporated into The Hamlyn Publishing Group. But over most of this period my editor for the books has been Robert Pearson, the former deputy editor of *Gardeners' Chronicle* (now known to a wide range of readers through his interesting weekly article in *The Sunday Telegraph*), with whom I have built up a close relationship. All in all not far short of two million copies of my books have been sold.

Quite a large slice of my life has gone into lecturing. The first I gave was to a Townswomen's Guild while I was at Derby. I won't forget that occasion for I was so nervous that I bought a small bottle of whisky and had several swigs of it to give me enough courage to go on the stage and talk. The occasion was brought back to me not so long ago when a party came to The Magnolias from Derby and two ladies in the party came up and said they remembered well this first lecture of mine.

That lecture led to talks to societies both in Derby and Shrewsbury. And then when I linked up with ICI I toured the whole of the British Isles. Two occasions spring to mind as outstanding; the Colston Hall in Bristol when three thousand eight hundred people

An article for *John Bull* magazine brought a meeting with that great broadcaster Richard Dimbleby in his mother's garden at Richmond, Surrey

The launching, in 1976, of *Percy Thrower's Guide to Good Gardening*, a Response Record giving 'month by month advice on garden care and cultivation'

turned up, and the Free Trade Hall in Manchester when three thousand five hundred attended. I went all over the place and I don't think I ever let my sponsors down by not arriving at the proper place at the correct time – though on a few occasions it was touch and go! Once I motored to Cheadle in Cheshire and looked in vain for the Town Hall in which I was to talk. No sign of it anywhere and when at last I asked someone I got the blunt reply: 'No Town Hall here, mate, are you sure you've got the right Cheadle? There's another one in Staffordshire, not far from Stoke-on-Trent.' I got out my letter from ICI and on it plainly enough was the address 'Cheadle, Staffordshire'. I was fifty miles away from that Cheadle and I'd got an hour. I did it with two minutes to spare! Another time I was going down to Horsham in Sussex and had just passed Birmingham when my windscreen shattered. I couldn't get it repaired so I left my car, jumped on a train to London, took a taxi across London to Victoria Station, another train to Horsham, and arrived once again just in the nick of time. On both occasions I went in to find a worried staff, wondering what they were going to do if no speaker turned up.

My association with ICI goes back some eighteen years or so and I have to acknowledge that it was the best contract I ever signed. ICI never used my name in conjunction with advertising for any of their products all the way through until the last few years when they have done so with my permission. I gave talks on their behalf, went to garden shops and centres, departmental stores and so on. A programme was drawn up every year promoting their products but I would get up on the stage or whatever and give my talk not mentioning one of them. ICI did not mind: their products were displayed at the time of my appearance and they were quite happy with the results. And so was I. It was through publicity from these lectures and with my television programmes that I began to be called 'Britain's Head Gardener'.

But despite all the attractions of the world of publicity and entertainment my heart still stayed – and always will stay – in the garden and among the plants I love. I have always striven to keep my two feet firmly on the ground. Whenever I have an inclination to feel big-headed about anything the words of an old friend of mine, Bill Carter, keep coming back to me. Bill was head gardener at Attingham Park, south-east of Shrewsbury and I used to go over to his place quite regularly. One day we were walking round the vegetable garden when he stopped, looked keenly at me, and said, 'D'ye know Percy, you're doing very well. You're broadcasting, doing some television, a bit of writing and earning a fair amount of money I expect . . .' I mumbled something to the effect that I supposed I was and he went on '. . . but there's one thing I want to say to you. You must always remember this – it takes a damn good horse to carry corn.'

The Magnolias

My house, The Magnolias, stands at six hundred feet above sea level just outside the village of Bomere Heath, six miles to the north-west of Shrewsbury. Why and how I decided to build myself a home and garden here is a curious story, one that started many years ago.

Shooting comes into it. As I mentioned earlier I learnt to handle a gun when still a lad with my father and shooting has remained one of my chief recreations. I first began to take it up seriously at Derby when I became the possessor of an old Belgian double-barrelled hammer gun for which I think I paid £3. I obtained permission to shoot rabbits on a farm just outside the town but later I rented a small shoot where the range was enlarged by the addition of a few pheasant, partridges, ducks and hares. Then when I came to Shrewsbury I got some rough shooting south-west of the town and later was allowed to shoot over a farm to the north-west – in the Bomere Heath neighbourhood. My companions at Shrewsbury for much of the shooting have been farmer John Whittingham and his brother Doug, who is not only my friend but my accountant.

I have done syndicate shooting but I prefer to go out with just a friend and the dogs for I consider it more sporting – the quarry I reckon has more than a fifty-fifty chance of getting away from us. I am quite happy if I come home with perhaps a hare, or a pheasant or a couple of rabbits – for I have had a good walk and enjoyed myself. At heart I suppose I remain a country lad.

The old Belgian gun is no longer in use by me. I had it when I came to Shrewsbury to live but one day I went to advise the managing director of the Sentinel Wagon Works (before Rolls Royce took them over) on his garden. This man noticed the gun in the boot of my car and warned me that hammer guns could be quite dangerous. I told him I was quite happy with it and in any case I was never likely to be able to afford something like a Purdey at around £1,000 or whatever the price was at that time. He then said, 'I may be able to help you,' and going indoors came back with an expensive-looking sporting gun. He explained that he had been out after rabbits one day and running out of cartridges had set about the rabbits with the stock of the gun, with the unfortunate result that the stock had broken. He had not bothered to have it repaired. He said to me, 'If you'd like the gun and have a proper stock put on it, you're welcome.' I took the gun to a shop in Shrewsbury who put on a nice walnut stock for £13 – and I am still using that gun at the present day. With it I can hold my own against all the Purdeys that some gentlemen of my acquaintance turn up with on the more formal shooting occasions.

About twenty years ago the owner of the farm next to the one over which I shot went bankrupt and his farm was put up for sale. His neighbour, who was John Whittingham, wanted to buy two of the fields to add to his land but they were not being sold separately. So I suggested we bought the farm between us: he could then have the two fields and we would sell off the rest of the farm and with luck make a profit. I proposed we should bid up to £13,000 but he thought £11,000 was plenty for it was, in his words, 'a wet farm, up to its knees in water.' On the day of the sale I was in London and when I got back and found that it had gone for £12,000 and that he had not bought it I was quite annoyed – for I was convinced we could have made a handsome profit. However, the buyer proved willing to resell and eventually John got his two fields for £110 an acre while two other fields adjoining, which were not so good, were sold off for £95 an acre. This left sixteen acres of rather rough land covered with a tangled mass of brambles and in the bottom of one field, below a dip, a pit covering nearly one-tenth of an acre.

The land was no good for farming but, on the other hand, it was excellent for shooting over. Meeting the owner one evening in the local I asked him how much he wanted. '£95 an acre,' he said. On the spur of the moment I offered him £75 and to my surprise he accepted my bid without further argument. Doug Whittingham and I bought the land jointly.

We decided to improve it so as to increase its value. We obtained drainage and ploughing up grants and brought in a bulldozer to level the ground by taking four feet off a knoll and using the subsoil from it to fill the large pit. The topsoil was spread back over. We grew barley for a year or two and then put it back to grass.

Out shooting over it one day, as we were lining up the guns along a hedge I suddenly found myself gazing at the familiar but always wonderful view. There was the Wrekin, Caer Caredoc, the Long Mynd, Stiperstones, Wenlock Edge and away beyond towards Ludlow I could just make out Brown Clee. Few views in England could rival this. I said to Doug who was beside me 'What a place to build a house?' and he replied quietly, 'Then why don't you?'

His remark set me thinking. I was due to retire as parks superintendent at Shrewsbury in about twelve years and the house we were living in, Quarry Lodge, went with the job. We would need somewhere to live.

It stayed on my mind all day and all that night. The next morning I took Connie with me and we went out to Bomere Heath, parked the car by the old broken-down gate that was the entrance to the property, climbed to the top of the high bank, admired the view and then I said to her: 'What about us building a house here?'

I think she was as taken aback as I had been when Doug Whittingham had said the same to me the day before. Her first reaction was, 'We've got a house, why do we want another?' I reminded her that it was a tied house and that in about a dozen years we would be looking for somewhere else to live. I added, 'And if I wait until then to make a garden I shall never live to see the benefit of it.' For at the back of my mind I wanted, like all real gardeners, to start a garden from scratch to my own design and make something I would be proud of.

We talked and talked about it and also consulted our three daughters. Finally we decided to build – and to get started on the project without any further delay.

Planning permission was the next move and as we wanted the house high up, almost on the skyline, we felt we might have difficulties in getting it. But this was 1962 and regulations were not so strict as they are today. The proposed site being adjacent to a farmhouse and several cottages, no objections were raised. If we had left it another three years we would have to have built the house at the bottom of the slope. Now we were to be six hundred feet up, exposed to the freshness of all the four winds and with a marvellous view.

We decided we did not want to spend more than £7,500 on the house. We had an architect draw up plans but when quotations were sought from builders on these plans the lowest tender was for £9,500. I refused to pay that amount, for I felt that it was not justified. So we scrapped the architect's plans and ourselves sketched out on paper just how we would like the house arranged. The slope of the ground was to the south so we opted for the kitchen, dining room and lounge to face that way and give a view across the hills. The rest of the house was planned around these three rooms.

That done I contacted a builder by the name of Bradley from the nearby village of Baschurch, a man who had a good reputation for the quality of his work. I asked him to take a look at our sketch and, if he was interested, to give a quotation. He put the rough sketch to scale and informed us that he would undertake the job for £7,000. That was more like it and I had no hesitation in accepting.

Later on we asked for a double garage instead of a single one, walling and terracing along the front and walling at the back, together with a cattle grid at the entrance and lamp posts up the drive – all as extras. In the end it cost us £8,000 which was certainly good value for money. By 1977 it is worth perhaps five times that amount.

We fenced in one and a half acres with hawthorn hedges to form the east and north boundaries. On the roadside was built a retaining wall of local red sandstone originally quarried only half a mile from here but in this case coming from an old farm building that had been pulled down somewhere in the locality. This was good, for it blended in with other walls round about and the last thing I wanted was for our place to stick out like a sore thumb. A beech hedge was planted inside the roadside wall and another one to separate the vegetable plots, greenhouses and other parts of the garden from the house. The drive was brought from the road round to the back (or north) of the house.

The boundaries and divisions decided upon, I made a rough sketch plan of what I wanted the garden to be. As you can imagine this was no easy task for there were so many things I wanted to do. And, of course, my ideas changed as the garden developed.

The soil around the house is gravelly, that on the slope leading down to the entrance gate and boundary hedge is a medium loam, while at the bottom of the garden it is a rather heavy clay which tends to become waterlogged in places in bad weather. All this had to be taken into account.

The pool and bog garden in its early stages

I meant to start on the garden in the winter of 1963 while the house was still being built, but for part of that winter the site was completely blocked by snow; at times we could not even get up the drive for the drifts. We have not had a winter like it since. But as soon as the snow cleared we started, changing this and that as we went along but all the time working basically from my rough sketch plan.

What did I want? First and foremost the design had to be informal: that was essential for the garden was right out in the country and I wanted it to fit into the Shropshire countryside. A formal garden would have been far too conspicuous so I kept away from straight lines. Island beds and the borders were irregularly shaped with trees and shrubs dotted around to create points of interest. Two small concrete rock pools were built as a focal point to the slope in front of the house. Designed to use rainwater from the roof, the first pool was cut into the bank halfway down the slope and a waterfall led into the other pool. An electric pump circulated the water. Round the two pools we put retaining walls and then the stones to make a rock garden. This provided a rock-water feature which is colourful for many months of the year, is easy to look

after and has the kind of informality which accords well with this modern age. The rainwater from the roof is piped to the pools.

That was the beginning of the garden, all carried out while the building of the house was going on. During this period the field grass was kept regularly cut with a rotary mower so that the finer grasses had a chance to develop and the turf did not become a mass of weeds.

I allowed myself eight years to develop the garden to its full potential; to get it just as I wanted it. I refrained from hurrying too much for I knew I would be continually changing my mind as the work progressed. But things happened faster than I expected, thanks in great part to the builder who became so interested in what I was attempting that he helped me on the rock garden and with concreting and installing the pump in the pools (for which I was particularly grateful, for I knew little about such matters). As the garden took shape I found myself wanting to see results so I suppose I worked harder and put in more hours of my spare time than I had originally intended. Anyway, in less than four years the garden was completed.

The pool and bog garden – now a mature feature

One thing I insisted on – no overhead wires; so when the drive was being made we put ducts underneath to take the water supply and the cables for the telephone and electricity. (This has the great advantage, apart from hiding the wires, that new cables can be put in without digging up a large area of the garden.)

We built a pergola. To me a pergola always has an old-world charm, and there is no need for them to take up too much room. Over it I planted the lovely white rose Madame Alfred Carrière; the carmine-pink thornless rose Zéphirine Drouhin; three clematis: Bees' Jubilee, Nelly Moser and Gypsy Queen; two Dutch honeysuckles (*Lonicera periclymenum belgica* and *L. p. serotina*), a passion flower (*Passiflora caerulea*), and a wisteria. The poles of the pergola (and also the poles on which I grow perpetual-flowering climbing roses in various places of the garden, for it is too exposed a site for standard roses) I put, on the advice of the builder, into drainpipes sunk into the ground to form a socket. Now when the bottom of a pole eventually rots all I have

111

to do is to take it out and replace it with a new one and the plants growing up the pergola or the separate poles are undisturbed.

The area at the top of the pool is one of the few places reserved for annual bedding

The whole garden, more or less, was planted with permanent plants so as to cut the recurring work to the minimum. I realized that when the time came for us to live at The Magnolias I would be older and perhaps not want to do a great deal of arduous physical work. So I used mainly trees, shrubs, roses, hardy border plants, alpines and so on, keeping summer bedding down to a minimum apart from a small piece around the top of the rock garden, in front of the terrace and at the back of the house.

What I learnt in making my new garden can perhaps

be summed up in something I wrote, soon after my garden was finished, in one of my books, *Everyday Gardening in Colour*, for the benefit of owners of new gardens. This was:

1. Sort out in your own mind the kind of garden features you want to have and consider carefully how these are going to relate to the size and physical surroundings of your plot.

2. When you are ready to start work put first things first and make sure that jobs which cannot be easily attended to later (like laying land drains, where these are necessary) are given precedence.

3. Do not rush your fences but plan the full development of the garden over four or five years if you have a

Trees form the backbone of the garden at The Magnolias and were among the first subjects to be planted

large area to cope with, less of course for smaller areas.

4. Make sure that the garden you design and develop is the kind you can enjoy over many years, and remember that it is the least pretentious layouts and plantings schemes which usually hold one's interest longest.

5. Always buy first-class plants from good nurseries. There is no profit in running a garden for plant invalids.

To return to The Magnolias; the hawthorn hedge on the field side boundary was allowed to grow up to seven or eight feet, which took about six years, and then I got a labourer from the adjoining farm to come in and pleach it. I had watched this man laying hedges and I saw that he was a true craftsman in this line, someone not easy to come by these days. And he did a first-class job on my hedge; today not even a dog can get through it, let alone children, and grazing cattle, which I often have in the adjoining field, are kept well out. It was planted five plants to the yard, a double row, three on the one side and two on the other, alternate in the row. The beech on the other hand were eighteen inches apart in a single row at the top of a bank. A Leyland cypress (x *Cupressocyparis leylandii*) hedge was planted by the side of the house to give protection from the prevailing south-west winds and the plants for this were put one yard apart and topped in their third year when they were six feet high. This cypress hedge also gave us privacy from the road, something we were to need later when television had made my name what is called a 'household' one and when on a Sunday the road outside would often be lined with cars and the occupants either watching me through binoculars or taking photographs.

The lawns on the north side of The Magnolias were grown from seed

All my lawns I developed from the original field grass with the exception of the areas adjoining the house where, wanting something tip-top, I rotavated, took out the never-ending stones (using them for making paths) and sowed a mixture of selected fine grasses. The grass on the bank was a three-year-old ley that the farmer had sown and with regular mowing while the building was going on it was amazing how the finer grasses came through and the coarse grass died out. We kept it mown, treated it with weedkiller, fed it with fertilizer and it made a reasonable hard-wearing lawn.

Greenhouses play an important part in supplying plants for the house and garden, and fruits for the table

At the back of the house in the north-west corner I put my greenhouses and frames. I eventually finished up with four houses, each different from the others. A sixteen-feet by eight-feet light alloy house divided into two sections has one section intended to be kept at a high temperature for the cultivation of those plants needing such conditions during the winter months and the other section is reserved for plants needing cooler conditions. (This was arranged to keep heating costs down for I could see the problem of increased fuel bills coming even then.) The second house, of cedar, measures thirteen feet by eight feet and is double glazed. This double glazing reduces the cost of heating to less than half that of the metal house. (Because of the high cost of manufacturing, these double-glazed houses are no longer on the market, but the same effect may be achieved by lining an ordinary greenhouse with thin polythene sheeting.) It has glass to the ground and was intended for tomatoes during the summer and chrysanthemums during the winter. (This has since been replaced with a house with removable sides to allow access for television cameras.) I also grow hippeastrums and orchids in the shade of the tomatoes and raise pelargoniums (geraniums), begonias, fuchsias, impatiens and other flowering plants. The third greenhouse, of the Dutch light type, is twenty feet long and ten feet wide and is made of cedar wood with glass to the ground. I fitted it up on the one side with an ash bed for the ring culture of tomatoes and for the accommodation of pot-grown chrysanthemums in the winter months, and on the other side with staging to

The first open day at The Magnolias in 1966

allow a wide range of plants to be grown both on and underneath the staging. My fourth greenhouse, eighteen feet by eight feet, is a lean-to against a west-facing wall. Constructed from a mixture of oak and metal it was erected later than the others. In it are fan-trained peaches on the wall with a vine along the top of the structure, while perpetual-flowering carnations in pots on the staging provide flowers for cutting throughout the year.

(Things have changed a little in my greenhouses recently. Since having my garden centre and nursery only a few miles away in Shrewsbury I have been cutting out the heating of my greenhouses at The Magnolias and taking the tender plants to overwinter in the warmth of the large greenhouses at the nursery. This makes a significant saving in fuel costs at home and also gives me a little less work to do there and, consequently, more time to spend on my nursery.)

After the greenhouses were built we decided to have a sun lounge in the corner formed by the kitchen and the back of the garden. But after it had been up a few years we found that we were using the front terrace to sit out on more than anywhere else and we realized that the sun lounge should have been over the French windows. So we had another built – in cedar wood with reinforced glass on top – and it has proved a real suntrap: even when a cold east wind is blowing it is very cosy.

On the east facing wall of the house is a Victoria plum tree which has never failed to fruit from the second year onwards. On the north-facing wall is a Morello cherry and under it are camellias that have gone up to nearly ten feet and flower every year. Honeysuckles cover the down pipes, climbing hydrangeas and peaches the front walls while *Cotoneaster horizontalis* and *Juniperus media pfitzeriana* are used to hide the manhole cover near the kitchen window.

As will be seen from the plan and key on page 124 the garden has a wide selection of trees, shrubs and hardy plants. One or two succumbed in the very dry summer of 1976 but in most cases these have been replaced by similar kinds.

I am sometimes asked what would I do differently if I were making The Magnolias over again? The answer is:

very little. Perhaps a few features of the house would be altered – it is said one has to build three houses before one is really satisfied. But it would be only minor things. As for the gardens I would do more or less the same all over again. I would certainly lay it out informally and use permanent plants to keep the recurring work down to the minimum. I suppose one could have less lawn, but lawns are very beautiful and the mowing these days can be quite easy work – though myself I prefer to walk with a mower even though it has a seat, because not only do I think I do a better job that way but the exercise does me good! Weeding, too, is not much of a problem with modern herbicides. For instance the long border on the left of the drive which is full of rhododendrons, azaleas and other ornamental trees and shrubs, has never had a fork in it since it was planted up. The weeds are kept down by spraying with paraquat weedkiller and this is used, too, in the fruit garden – it certainly saves a great deal of unnecessary labour.

Right from the start the garden was planned with a view to its being suitable for television with wide hard paths and plenty of room for the cameramen to manoeuvre. We started televising even while the garden was being made.

And, of course, as a result of television the garden has become very well known. We certainly discovered how well when we began opening the garden in aid of charity. The first time we did so (it was for the Gardeners' Royal Benevolent Society and the Gardeners' Benevolent Fund) over five thousand people turned up and we had a great problem with car parking. We also opened it for the Red Cross and other organizations. The best Sunday of all was one in July 1970, but luckily on this occasion the owner of the field opposite our place allowed us to use it for a car park. By mid afternoon one could hardly see the grass of the field because of motor vehicles on it. They included some forty coaches. We admitted seven-and-a-half thousand people and then ran out of tickets. But at the end of the day we worked out that over nine-and-a-half thousand had passed through the garden. The general average since has been between five and six thousand and the garden, by 1976, had

In the garden at The Magnolias

earned for charity something in excess of £20,000. Yet, despite the large crowds, surprisingly little damage has been done to the garden; I can go round on a Sunday evening after an open day and though the grass may be trodden flat and worn in places, hardly an empty cigarette packet or a used ticket will be found. Which says a lot for gardening folk; they're a fine crowd.

On these occasions as much fuss is made over our black Labrador, Whisky, as over the plants and the garden, but she takes all this in her stride. She is thirteen now and the last of four dogs we have had since we were at Derby. It was there that we became the owners of Mick, the result of an encounter between one of the parks employee's black cocker spaniel and an old English sheepdog. Mick was a first-rate gun dog and would run through any fence or thicket in the course of a shoot. After him came a pedigree black and white cocker spaniel which was more suited to the show bench than shooting, and then, in 1955, our first black Labrador, Sue.

The breed had been a favourite of mine since I had seen Grandfather Dunnett's Labrador on duck-shooting expeditions when I was a boy. I came upon Sue quite by chance. Peggy Harper, an assistant producer of women's TV programmes, was complaining one day that the black Labrador she had was really much too big for her flat; it was now ten months old and she felt that she would have to find it a home before it became much older. I said I was interested and without further ado I set out to look at the dog. Sue was rather an agitated animal when I first saw her but as soon as we got out to the car she made a tremendous fuss of me and we remained firm friends; I was surprised to find that, in spite of her early upbringing, she was an excellent gun dog.

The dog we have at the present time, Whisky, came to us from my old friend John Whittingham. John was the owner of Tinky, the runt of a litter of Sue's pups, and one day Tinky got out and mated with, as luck would have it, a first-class pedigree golden Labrador. I took a liking to the runt of Tinky's litter: a black pup with long whiskers – so long in fact that my daughter, Ann, decided that the pup should be called 'Whiskers'. I thought about

Margaret with the family's first dog, Mick

Whisky – an invaluable garden
companion

this for a while and said that I was more fond of whisky than whiskers and so 'Whisky' she was called – and she has been with us ever since, proving herself of real worth as a garden companion and gun dog.

I have always been keen on dogs and also cats but even so I had refused the girls' frequent requests for a cat on the grounds that cats couldn't travel like dogs, and anyway as we had a dog we didn't want a cat and that was that.

This situation was accepted, until one day in 1971 when a painter, who was painting the lampposts in the drive, came up to the house and said he had just found a small Siamese kitten. It was all skin and bone and, in his own words, 'on its last gasp'. He had found it under the cattle grid, where it had obviously been for some days, and on inspection it seemed to have a broken leg. Connie fed and nursed it all that day and I agreed to take it to the vet the following morning. The vet's assistant was quite taken with the kitten, which she said was a lilac-point Siamese, so I suggested that she might like to keep it. I came back home quite pleased with myself and was met by the girls who, after I had said that I had given the kitten away, told me I was cruel and mean and that they wanted to look after the poor little thing. I gave in and fetched the kitten back. In spite of advertisements being placed in the paper nobody claimed him and Ming, as he came to be known, has now taken over the house and me as well!

Finally, why did we call the new house The Magnolias? Well, writing as I have for *Amateur Gardening* over many years, when I started making my garden I told my readers about it and asked for ideas for a name. All sorts of names were sent in – one I remember was Thrower's Patch. But the majority were in favour of a flower name and perhaps somewhat strangely, magnolias were top of the list. So The Magnolias it became. With a name like that magnolias just had to grow well here. Luckily they did, and we have more than twenty flourishing today. Another strange thing: after we had moved to The Magnolias I discovered that the village of Bomere Heath has a Magnolia Close, but why it is so named I don't know.

A Plan of the Garden at The Magnolias

KEY TO PLAN
1. *Cupressus macrocarpa lutea* (a golden form of the Monterey cypress)
2. *Malus eleyi* (flowering crab)
3. *Chamaecyparis lawsoniana* (Lawson cypress)
4. *Chamaecyparis lawsoniana* (Lawson cypress)
5. *Cupressocyparis leylandii* (Leyland cypress)
6. *Chamaecyparis lawsoniana* (Lawson cypress)
7. *Eucalyptus gunnii*
8. *Ligustrum ovalifolium* (golden privet)
9. Trees on northern boundary – *Pinus sylvestris* (Scots pine) interplanted with silver birch to contrast the white stems of the latter with the dark background provided by the pines
10. *Eucalyptus dalrympleana*
11. *Prunus* Shirotae (Japanese flowering cherry)
12. *Magnolia kobus*
13. *Thuja occidentalis* Rheingold
14. *Hamamelis mollis*
15. Walnut tree

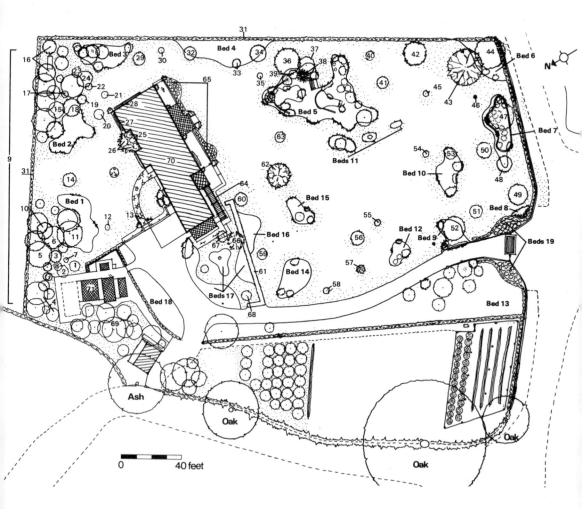

0   40 feet

16 *Larix decidua* (larch)
17 *Eucalyptus gunnii*
18 *Prunus* Hisakura (Japanese flowering cherry)
19 *Chamaecyparis lawsoniana* (Lawson cypress)
20 *Chamaecyparis lawsoniana aurea* (golden-yellow form of Lawson cypress)
21 *Ilex aquifolium pyramidalis* (conical form of common holly)
22 *Prunus* Amanogawa (Japanese flowering cherry)
23 *Syringa vulgaris* Charles X (variety of common lilac)
24 *Ligustrum ovalifolium aureum* (golden privet)
25 Camellias: J. C. Williams, Mary Christian, Francis Hanger and varieties of *Camellia japonica*
26 Covering manhole cover: *Cotoneaster horizontalis* and *Juniperus media pfitzeriana*
27 Morello cherry, on north-facing wall
28 Victoria plum, on east-facing wall
29 *Cupressocyparis leylandii* (Leyland cypress)
30 *Ilex altaclarensis* Golden King
31 Quickthorn hedge on east and north boundary
32 *Liriodendron tulipifera* (tulip tree)
33 *Chamaecyparis lawsoniana* (Lawson cypress)
34 *Prunus* Cheal's Weeping (flowering cherry)
35 *Hamamelis mollis*
36 *Salix chrysocoma* (golden weeping willow)
37 *Pinus ayacahuite*
38 *Phormium tenax* (New Zealand flax)
39 Bamboo
40 *Thuja plicata*
41 *Metasequoia glyptostroboides*
42 *Prunus subhirtella autumnalis* (winter-flowering cherry)
43 *Salix chrysocoma* (golden weeping willow)
44 *Pinus sylvestris* (Scots pine)
45 *Cedrus libani* (Cedar of Lebanon)
46 Yucca
47 *Prunus* Shirofugen (Japanese flowering cherry)
48 *Pinus sylvestris* (Scots pine)
49 *Crataegus oxyacantha* Paul's Scarlet (double red hawthorn)
50 *Malus sargentii* (flowering crab)
51 *Liquidambar stryaciflua*
52 *Prunus cerasifera pissardii* (purple-leaved plum)
53 *Picea glauca*
54 *Ginkgo biloba* (maidenhair tree)
55 *Prunus* Amanogawa (Japanese flowering cherry)
56 *Prunus veitchii*
57 *Cortaderia selloana* (pampas grass)
58 *Ilex aquifolium argenteomarginata*
59 *Cedrus atlantica glauca pendula*
60 *Laburnum vossii*
61 Hedge of *Cupressocyparis leylandii* (Leyland cypress)
62 *Prunus* Cheal's Weeping (flowering cherry)
63 *Magnolia soulangiana*
64 Pergola clothed with: climbing rose Madame Alfred Carrière, climbing rose Zéphirine Drouhin, *Clematis* Bees' Jubilee, *C.* Nellie Moser, *C.* Gypsy

Queen, *Lonicera periclymenum belgica* (early Dutch honeysuckle), *L. p. serotina* (late Dutch honeysuckle) and *Passiflora caerulea* (passion flower)
65 Floribunda roses – Vera Dalton
66 *Betula pendula youngii* (Young's weeping birch)
67 *Acer japonicum aconitifolium*
68 *Chamaecyparis lawsoniana*
69 *Acer pseudoplatanus brilliantissimum* (sycamore). The trees in this part of the garden provide protection and privacy, and also include *Pinus sylvestris* (Scots pine), silver birches and *Cupressocyparis leylandii*
70 House
71 Greenhouse and frames

PLANTS IN BEDS

Informal Island Bed 1: Shrubs, shrub roses, hardy fuchsias and herbaceous perennial plants, with a larch immediately behind them
Informal Bed 2: Rhododendrons, including miniature kinds. Mollis azaleas and *Rhododendron luteum* (syn. *Azalea pontica*), interplanted with ericas
Informal Bed 3: Shrubs, including *Cotoneaster salicifolius, Buddleia davidii* Peace, *Prunus cerasifera pissardii* and *Forsythia* Lynwood to give shelter from east winds
Informal Bed 4: Shrub roses
Bed 5: Rock and water feature
Bed 6: Hydrangeas, herbaceous perennial plants and shrubs
Bed 7: A raised bed with *Prunus* Shirofugen, rhododendrons (large and miniature), azaleas and lilies
Bed 8: Clematises trained over wire
Bed 9: Deciduous azaleas (Ghent and Mollis varieties) underplanted with ericas
Bed 10: Herbaceous perennial plants with some shrubs
Beds 11: Outcrops of rock surrounded by ericas which provide a succession of colour throughout the year. Pernettyas are grown here, too, and there is a specimen of *Betula papyrifera* (paper birch) in the larger bed
Bed 12: *Magnolia soulangiana*, ericas, azaleas and other shrubs as well as herbaceous perennial plants
Bed 13: Flowering trees and flowering and other ornamental shrubs. These include *Magnolia soulangiana, M. s. lennei, M. s. alba, Eucryphia nymansensis*, hibiscuses, *Viburnum bodnantense* and the Japanese flowering cherry, *Prunus* Ukon
Bed 14: *Magnolia stellata* at corner, and the rest of the planting consisting of other shrubs and hardy border plants
Bed 15: Hardy fuchsias and hardy border plants
Bed 16: Hardy border plants
Beds 17: Floribunda roses
Bed 18: Hybrid tea and floribunda roses
Beds 19: Floribunda rose Border Coral

Man of Business

As time went on my thoughts increasingly turned to what I should do when I retired as parks superintendent of Shrewsbury. Television, radio, writing and lecturing, together with my garden at The Magnolias would no doubt continue to account for a good many hours each week but I felt that I would like to have some kind of horticultural business of my own to attend to. Above all the idea of a garden centre appealed to me.

Garden centres are something comparatively new in British horticulture. They began, I understand, in the fifties in America and put in an appearance over here a few years later. Since then they have almost revolutionized gardening. They are more or less the supermarkets or hypermarkets of the industry, but different in that many are leisure centres as well – places where a whole family can go and enjoy themselves. Most of them are set away from the centres of large towns and cater chiefly for motor-borne customers.

Apart from their easy access for car customers the main factor that has contributed to their success has been the development of the container-grown plant. Traditionally, most hardy trees, shrubs and herbaceous plants have been lifted and sold bare-root during what I term the orthodox planting season, the dormant months of October to March. This was my teaching when starting gardening as a mere lad. But it is a bad period, for gardening conditions are at their worst and the plants, for the most part, are looking their least attractive. No one had attempted to produce a wide range of hardy plants to sell throughout the year until the early 1950s, when nurserymen in America and Australia began growing plants in old tin cans which, while adding little to the cost of the plants, did enable year-round

With Ming, the stray who came to stay

127

selling to take place. Later black polythene containers became popular.

Not all the places that are called, or call themselves, garden centres are worthy of the name. But the best are very good and an established one still in the top class is one that I was involved in right from the start at Syon Park.

It happened this way. In 1967 ICI asked me to go to Syon Park to meet the Duke of Northumberland and to give an opinion as to whether I considered his gardens suitable for turning into a national garden centre where all that was best in British horticulture could be put on show. ICI would be backing it.

Syon Park is a two hundred-acre estate only eight

The Great Conservatory, Syon Park

miles from Hyde Park yet so tucked away on the banks of the Thames near Brentford that one can imagine oneself to be in the heart of the countryside, were it not for the constant drone of planes passing over from nearby Heathrow Airport. Syon House has had a long and colourful history, both horticultural and otherwise. Originally the site of a monastery, its first gardens were designed in the sixteenth century by William Turner, physician to the Duke of Somerset and a keen botanist. Some of the present trees are thought to have been planted by him but most of his work was swept away later by the famous landscaper 'Capability' Brown who also stocked the estate with almost every foreign tree and shrub that could be obtained at that time. This collection has been added to regularly in the years since. Between 1820 and 1830 a conservatory – at that time the largest in Europe – was erected and this, filled with exotic plants of all descriptions, put Syon even more on the horticultural map.

By the time I went to Syon, however, the gardens were neglected and the lakes and woodlands overgrown and untidy. Yet I saw that its site and amenities certainly held the potential for a large garden centre providing sufficient money was forthcoming for extensive redevelopment.

I reported to this effect and Plant Protection Ltd., a subsidiary of ICI, leased fifty acres from the Duke and together they formed a company called The Gardening Centre. A board of directors which included among others Capt. Phillip Culmer as the Duke's representative and myself was set up. Jim Middleton was appointed horticultural manager.

As far as possible the landscape was left undisturbed but the main lake was cleaned out, edged by an eight-foot high western bank to prevent flooding from the Thames and stocked with a fine collection of water and moisture-loving plants. The woodland area behind it was given over to ornamental trees, shrubs and herbaceous plants. The place known as Old England (reputed to be where Caesar crossed the Thames in 54BC) was planted up with heaths and heathers. Further west a series of planned gardens were installed to demonstrate

129

ideas on planting for every size plot from a window box to a large country garden. To the north of the lake the latest in tools, greenhouses, garden buildings, fences, fountains, furniture, fertilizers, machinery and every other kind of gardening requisite were given space for permanent display.

Where the old Tudor gardens had once stood a six-acre rose garden was laid out with ten thousand roses. The nineteenth-century conservatory was taken over to house a comprehensive collection of house plants, carnations, fuchsias, orchids and similar plants. The garden outside the conservatory was bordered with spring and summer bedding plants while the old riding stables were converted into offices for the selling area and accommodation for students.

It was a hectic time with machinery and men everywhere, the lake being dredged, roads and paths being constructed and it seemed in the early months of 1968 that the place would never be ready for the official opening scheduled for June. We pushed, kicked and struggled and eventually we got it right just on target, and I had the honour of escorting the Queen Mother when she arrived to open the Centre.

As I said, the aim of the Centre was to help the horticultural trade of the country. Syon's position between Heathrow Airport and central London made it a convenient centre for manufacturers and nurserymen from all over Britain. To help with business transactions a conference hall, exhibition areas, film areas, meeting rooms and catering facilities were provided.

Altogether some £500,000 was invested in the Centre, the major stockholders being the Duke of Northumberland and ICI but with some twenty per cent. of the capital coming from outside sources in Europe and America.

The opening months of the Centre were very successful for the place was a novelty – nothing like it had been seen before. But before long I realized that all was not well. It was not the fault of the Centre itself, rather, to my mind, it lay in the employment of too many non-productive staff – advertising managers, sales managers and so on – which was making the concern top heavy and, more

The opening of The Garden Centre at Syon Park. The Queen Mother is accompanied by Sir Peter Allen (then chairman of ICI) and the author

serious, unprofitable. I tried to put this view over at board meetings but with little success. As time went by costs continually increased and with the number of visitors slowly dropping it became difficult to show a profit. Eventually ICI saw the red light and pulled out. Although another group stepped in for a while they were no more successful and finally the Duke took over the running himself. Soon after this happened I resigned as a director.

Syon Park remains a fine garden centre; certainly one of the best selling centres in the country. The Duke got his gardens, lakes and grounds put in good order so he did not do too badly out of it, though in recent years he has had to bring in other attractions such as a transport and vintage car museum to keep the Centre viable. I remain convinced, however, that if it had been handled differently The Gardening Centre at Syon Park would have enjoyed a much more prosperous life.

However, this experience did not put me off wanting a garden centre of my own. Quite the reverse in fact – I was more than ever of the opinion that a centre run with the right knowledge behind it and accompanied by modern methods of promotion could be a great success. I continued to keep my eyes open for something suitable – for preference a nursery that could be enlarged into a garden centre. One day in 1970 I was at Dobbies the Edinburgh seed firm to open a garden centre for Waterers who had taken the firm over when, in the course of conversation, Captain Barnes of Waterers asked me what I knew about Murrells of Shrewsbury. I knew Murrells, of course: they were a long-established nursery firm with a high reputation especially for their roses which included an enviable collection of the old-fashioned kinds. I had known old Edwin Murrell and his brother, and I was acquainted with the present Miss Murrell who was in charge of the nursery and Leslie, her brother, who had a garden shop in the town. The original Portland Nurseries had been sold for building some five years previous and a new nursery set up on a site outside the town, on the Shrewsbury bypass. I enquired of Captain Barnes as to the reason for his enquiry and I was most surprised to hear that Murrells was for sale. Though I lived in Shrewsbury it was the first I had heard of it. My reaction was to say, 'Then you must buy it,' for I wanted to see it stay as a horticultural concern under a good owner. But I was told that Waterers were not in a position at that time to consider it. This set me thinking.

It was, of course, just the sort of place I was looking for and, what was more, it was in my home town. I would be unlikely to get another chance like this – if only I could raise the money. I asked Captain Barnes if he minded me making enquiries when I got back and he told me to go ahead and wished me luck.

I couldn't get back to Shrewsbury quick enough. I went immediately to my accountant and told him the news, only to find that he already knew about it, and that, in fact, one of his partners was handling the transaction. But he also added that someone else was interested – a person with plenty of money – one Duncan Murphy whose father had just sold his Wrekin Brewery and was looking for another business in which to invest his money.

Now I knew Duncan Murphy's father quite well; in fact we had had many a drink together. And I knew the son was interested in gardening though he had had no business experience of it. So when my accountant suggested that a meeting might be mutually beneficial I was quite agreeable. We met in the accountant's office and Duncan Murphy at once declared that he was interested in buying the property whereupon I told him that I was not in a position to bid against a man who had just sold a brewery. However, if he would consider an equal partnership with him contributing the greater share of the money and me providing some capital but in addition the know-how of running such a business, then I was his man. Within ten minutes we had reached agreement – we were partners. In the event we paid £450 an acre for forty acres: it seemed a lot of money in 1970 but it has proved a bargain.

The new Portland Nurseries are on the side of the Shrewsbury bypass, the A5, a very busy road – ideal for the introduction of a garden centre. It had an established entrance on to the bypass and we obtained planning permission to widen this entrance and also to put in a car park and start a garden centre.

We retained the collection of old-fashioned roses that Miss Murrell had kept intact. And we also kept all the old staff who wanted to stay, for Miss Murrell had always been good to her staff and had asked us to look after them. The catalogue, a very comprehensive one, was continued and later we added to it, increasing the range of flowering and ornamental trees and bushes, shrubs, conifers and climbers as well as fruit trees and bushes. But more and more we turned our attention to container-grown trees, shrubs, roses and plants though, nevertheless, in spite of the rising costs of packing and despatching we have kept quite a large number of all these for lifting during the winter and spring when they can be sent to arrive in good condition anywhere in the country, even though transport costs are now rising.

We now grow some one hundred and fifty thousand roses a year which is pretty good going. We bring in a Dutch expert to do the budding and it is quite a sight to watch him working with two men hoeing out in front, two lads following behind to do the tying up and four other men preparing the budwood to keep him going. He puts on over four thousand buds a day and we aim to have budding finished by the time of the Shrewsbury Flower Show which takes place usually in the second week of August. We do three thousand standard roses which we make a point of budding first. We also propagate most of our own shrubs; at first we used a mist propagator for this but one day I was at Plant Protection's Research Station at Fernhurst in Sussex and saw carnations, chrysanthemums and several shrub species being rooted very successfully with just a covering of polythene sheeting over a heated bench. We had had quite a lot of trouble with our mist propagation unit what with furring up and so on, so when I came back I switched off the entire apparatus and substituted polythene sheeting over beds with cable heating underneath the sand. We get better rooting under this than we ever did and the cost is a good deal lower.

We raise about one hundred thousand shrubs and climbers a year from cuttings, including forty thousand conifers. The only things we buy in are rhododendrons, azaleas, magnolias, pieris, hamamelis, *Hydrangea paniculata* and maiden fruit trees – mostly from Holland. The maiden trees we grow on into bushes, cordons, half standards and standards on the various rootstocks. Fan-trained trees we buy in and these have already been established.

Our customers come from all parts of the United Kingdom and even from overseas. We have a sign outside, 'Percy Thrower's Garden and Leisure Centre' and such is the power of television and other media that many a person who has never heard of the Garden Centre will recognize the name as they pass by and often turn round

Outside the garden centre at Shrewsbury

at the next roundabout and come back. And because I speak and write about many different plants, visitors to the Centre expect to be able to find them all there. That means it is necessary to keep a wider range and a bigger stock than the average garden centre. Usually in a programme when I mention a plant that is rare I make a point of saying that it may be difficult, perhaps impossible, to obtain. For the same reason a few plants we raise in the nursery are too rare to go into our catalogue. If I were to mention I had a stock of any rare plant it would be sold out in no time and we would have to make our excuses to those customers we were not able to supply. We therefore keep such plants for people who come and ask specifically for them.

The garden centre has certainly helped to bring extra trade to Murrells of Shrewsbury. It has also extended considerably the season for trading. At one time nursery trade was almost all done in the winter; sending out trees, shrubs, plants and so on from catalogue orders. But with the advent of container-grown plants it means that the till rings all the year round instead of just during the winter months. The garden centre also has great advantages for the ordinary gardener; he no longer has to buy on a recommendation or a description in a catalogue or book, he can now see these 'names' growing in containers and often in flower as well so that he can decide whether he likes them or not. He can also find out just how big a plant grows, where it is best suited, the kind of soil it prefers and if it is likely to do well in his particular district. He doesn't have to wait till winter for it; he can buy it and plant it out at a time when it is much more comfortable for gardening: no longer is it necessary to do the planting in the cold, murky days of winter when the soil can be cold, wet and sticky. And, again, he is more likely to be successful with a plant from a container where there is no disturbance to the roots than he is from one that is lifted from the nursery with bare roots. The average person is impatient: now he can take a rose or a shrub home in flower, plant it in the garden and get immediate effect. And with fruit trees – he can even carry home an apple tree with apples on it if he so desires. Provided, of course, that the basic

HOL
SPRI

PERCY
(FLOF

SPECIAL MIDL

principles of handling container-grown plants: watering before taking the plant out of the container, mixing peat with the soil before planting, watering the plant after planting, making it firm in the soil, not planting too deeply, are adhered to.

Also in a garden centre a person can inspect all the various sundries – tools, machines, equipment and so on – that help to make gardening easier and better. It should be, too, to my mind, a place where the whole family can come in and browse around. We advertise: 'Come and enjoy a walk round in pleasant surroundings'; and we mean it. They may buy nothing or very little but if they have enjoyed walking round a garden centre they will no doubt come back again someday. And with the shorter working week people are going to have more time for gardening; already it is the most popular leisure occupation and one of the greatest of all hobbies.

Another facet of business opened up for me one evening about thirteen years ago when I was having a quiet half-pint in the 'Hand and Diamond' just over the Welsh border near here with an old friend, Harold Sleigh. Harold, who ran a travel agency in Shrewsbury, suddenly asked, 'Would you be interested in earning a few coppers on the side?' I replied, 'I've never been too proud to do that,' and he went on to outline a scheme he had thought up to take people interested in gardening on trips abroad. To begin with he had the Dutch bulb fields in mind. My job would be to go with the party and talk about the horticultural aspects. What did I think of the idea? I thought it a good one and agreed to go in with him. We began taking parties of about eighty to Holland for four-day trips. We flew in Derby Airways DC 4s using Birmingham and Castle Donington airports. I would go with some of the party and Harold and his assistant, Brian Bass, with the remainder. We did the usual Dutch run-round – Keukenhof, Delft china works, cheesemaking, bulb fields, a trip up the Amsterdam canals at night and so forth. Everyone seemed to enjoy it and it was certainly good value for money. But then a large tour operator got in on the act and also began hiring Derby Airways (or rather Midland Airways as they had now become) and we began to find that if an

137

aeroplane broke down it would always be us that suffered. We would find ourselves in the position of having dear old ladies at the airport who had never flown before when it would be announced that there was to be a half an hour's delay in the flight. We would provide them with a glass of brandy to make up for the wait, but then after another half an hour's delay they wanted a second brandy. After a further two hours' delay they felt entitled to a meal – and looked to us to provide it. After several of these experiences we decided enough was enough: if we could not do the job properly we wouldn't do it at all.

So that finished, but almost directly afterwards the owners of the Greek ship *Arkadia* expressed an interest in conducted garden cruises farther afield. This was a much bigger undertaking than the previous tours so, in cooperation with Harold Sleigh, I formed Percy Thrower Floral Tours which had its headquarters in Shrewsbury. We first of all did eight cruises with the *Arkadia* to places such as Tenerife, Las Palmas, Madeira and Gibraltar taking one hundred and fifty on each, then became more ambitious and chartered the Union Castle

Lifejacket inspection on board the *Arkadia*

Bargaining with a native in Tangiers

Bargaining with a native in Tangiers

ships, the *Reina del Mar* and *S.A. Vaal*, for tours to South Africa. Later came cruises with the *Q.E.2* (with these I gave gardening talks in the ship's cinema and they were always packed), the *Canberra* and the *Blenheim*. We hope to do plenty more yet.

Considering that as a young man I never went, or even dreamt of going, beyond the shores of the British Isles, I have certainly made up for it in recent years. And in 1976 we made a private trip to Canada to visit Connie's sister Mabel in Newfoundland.

Now I have ambitions to go to the United States, New Zealand, Australia and Scandinavia. But even if I never get to these places I feel I have now done my fair share of travelling about the world.

Favourites of a Lifetime

I have always looked upon myself as a perfectionist: in my early days I was taught that only the best was good enough, and that principle has stayed with me the whole of my life.

Naturally through the years I have found myself liking some plants better than others but, as with a family of children, it is best not to show too much favour to any particular one. When I walk round my garden I like almost all of what I see, which is quite natural for did I not choose them myself? Yet if I were forced to make a choice I know that certain ones would have to be retained irrespective of what happened to the others.

One would be the greenhouse cyclamen: this must be reckoned high on my list of favourite flowers. My father prided himself on the way he could grow them and at Derby Parks John Maxfield the head gardener was a specialist in them so I was set a high standard right from my early days. They give a wonderful display from autumn right through until March or April in a greenhouse. I like to sow the seeds, not in December or January, but in the previous May or June so as to give them at least eighteen months from sowing to flowering. In this way I get a larger plant with more flowers and the flowers last longer than those produced by a shorter period of cultivation. The seed should be spaced out evenly on the surface of a pan of seed compost and covered lightly with sifted compost which is then firmed. Cover the pan with a pane of glass and a sheet of newspaper to prevent the rapid drying out of the compost, wipe the condensation from the glass every day and as soon as the seed germinates remove the coverings. Then stand the pan in a warm shaded part of the greenhouse. When the seedlings are large enough to handle lift them carefully and prick them out about one-and-a-half inches apart. (Some seeds take longer than others to germinate so don't throw away the seed pan until it is apparent that most of the seedlings that are likely to, have appeared.) Before the seedlings get overcrowded pot them singly into three-inch pots and stand them on a shelf to get as much light as possible in a temperature of 10 to 13°C (50 to 55°F). As the pots fill with roots transfer the plants into larger pots in which they will flower.

Cyclamens like cool conditions in summer and the best place then is a cold frame with some shading from the sun. Give plenty of space between the pots and feed the plants with a suitable fertilizer. Towards the end of September get the plants back into a frost-proof greenhouse and remove any dead leaves and green slime from the pots. Allow plenty of ventilation and on warm days damp the floor and staging to maintain a humid atmosphere. As the weather becomes colder keep a steady temperature of at least 10°C (50°F) at night. The first flowers appear in the autumn and I like to remove these until the main flush of flowers develops, and when these begin to fade I remove them, too. The best plants may be kept for a second year.

Begonias of the Gloire de Lorraine type were another of my father's favourites; we also had plenty of them at Windsor and at Darley Abbey Park in Derby.

Lorraine begonias which are fibrous-rooted and winter-flowering are more graceful than the tuberous begonias and the stems are more wiry. To obtain young basal growths for cuttings the stems are cut back after flowering within a few inches of their base. Kept in warm conditions new shoots soon develop and these can be removed in February as cuttings. A suitable rooting mixture consists of equal parts of moist peat and coarse sand, well mixed. Each cutting is prepared by trimming the base just below a leaf joint and removing the lower leaves. The cuttings should be about four inches long and several can be placed round the edge of a three-inch pot and the pot placed in a propagating frame at a temperature of 18°C (65°F). After rooting the cuttings

The Lorraine begonias can be relied upon to give a delicate display of colour in the winter months

Hanging baskets are an ideal way of displaying fuchsias to best effect

are first put into three-inch pots, I suggest using John Innes No. 1 potting compost, and if the temperature in the frame is slightly reduced, a moist atmosphere maintained and some shading from strong sunshine given, growth will be rapid. Final potting is into five- or six-inch containers.

At the Royal Gardens, Windsor there was a corridor where fuchsias of many varieties covered the sides. This was always a wonderful sight and I think my love of fuchsias stems from that time. The fuchsia is such a versatile plant it will grow in a greenhouse, up a wall, as a pot plant or standard, is ideal for window-boxes, tubs and containers on the terrace or patio, and for hanging baskets. At The Magnolias I have gone in for the hardy fuchsias which flower continuously from late June right through until November sometimes if the frosts hold off. At the top of the rock garden I have the purple and red Corallina with its rather prostrate habit; mauve and red Tom Thumb, compact and free flowering; purple and red Mrs Popple, rather tall, and one of the more vigorous of the hardy fuchsias; the mauve and red Margaret Blake, not quite as vigorous as Mrs Popple; Pumila, a small one for the rock garden; O.K., another dwarf with small leaves but full of flower through all the summer; Dunrobin Bedder, a good one for the rock garden or the front of a border; the mauve and red Susan Travis; Madame Cornelissen with white and carmine semi-double blooms, and last, but certainly not least, the white and red Alice Hoffmann, which in some parts of the country will grow to two-and-a-half feet or more but here in Shropshire doesn't go above two feet, though it is free flowering and showy.

As a garden centre we exhibit each year at the Shrewsbury Flower Show and in 1974 we put up a large stand of fuchsias which not only gained us a cup but also the award for the best exhibit in the show. It was very rewarding to gain an award at this illustrious show with which I have been connected for so many years. We put on more than eighty varieties – in the form of standards, hanging baskets, bush plants and trailing plants and also made a fuchsia garden. In all we used over four hundred plants.

The culture of the hardy varieties of fuchsia consists of planting in October or April in ordinary well-drained soil in sheltered positions in sun or partial shade. Protect in winter with layers of dry litter or sharp cinders over the crowns of the plants and in April, if any of the top growth has been damaged by frost, cut it off. (This may necessitate cutting back to ground level in some cases, but the plants usually throw up strong new shoots from the crowns and these flower the same year.) Propagation is best carried out by putting two- to three-inch long young shoots into sandy soil in spring or summer at a temperature of around 16°C (60°F).

Roses always give me a sense of achievement and satisfaction. At The Magnolias I planted plenty because they need the minimum amount of attention and are more or less permanent, thus keeping down the recurring work. Shrub roses are particularly good for this – even more so than the hybrid teas and floribundas. On the pillars I used the perpetual-flowering climbers – Autumn Sunlight, with its brilliant flame, well-shaped flowers throughout the season; Pink Perpetue, a star performer with carmine buds opening to a clear china rose; Casino, with its classic, richly scented, hybrid-tea blooms in clear yellow shading to lemon; Royal Gold, a deep yellow; Golden Showers, large, semi-double blooms in clusters forming, as its name implies, a golden shower; Parkdirektor Riggers, a fine splash of almost blood-red colour; Parade, with scented double flowers of a bright deep pink – this is one of the most free-flowering perpetual climbers I have ever planted; Galway Bay, unfading carmine and seemingly always in bloom; Schoolgirl, on its own in climbing roses for its soft copper-orange colour, and hosts of others. These perpetual-flowering climbing roses do give so much more satisfaction than those that only flower once. The rather wilder-looking wichuraiana roses such as American Pillar, Dorothy Perkins, Hiawatha and Minnehaha give a good display but they can't really compete with the perpetuals particularly as they have a susceptibility to mildew when grown on walls. Aftercare of the perpetual flowering roses is merely a matter of removing a few of the oldest shoots every year thus keeping up a rotation and a constant production of new growth.

Since taking over the wonderful collection of roses of Murrells of Shrewsbury I am learning to appreciate more than ever the charm of many of the shrub and other old-fashioned roses. We try and exhibit them at shows and my daughter Margaret uses them in many flower arrangements. There are so many that it is difficult to make a choice but certain ones I would always go for: La Reine Victoria, for example, when I look at the shape and colour of this soft lilac-pink Bourbon rose I always think of an old Dutch painting with a rose lying on the table beside an arrangement of flowers. Another I love is Mme Pierre Oger which has leaves with crinkled edges and cup-shaped blooms that remind me of the old-fashioned shell flowers and which change from white to deep rose according to the weather: it too, is a Bourbon

The pergola at The Magnolias is now well covered with clematis and roses. Here, Zéphirine Drouhin receives some attention

rose, a descendant of an accidental cross at the end of the eighteenth century between the China and Damask roses on the island of Reunion.

I am fond, too, of many varieties of *Rosa rugosa*, descendants of a wild rose of China and the Far East where it has been grown since the beginning of the twelfth century. Vigorous and hardy they will grow in almost any part of the country, even by the sea. They are fairly continuous in their flowering and with many of them such as Frau Dagmar Hartopp, *alba*, *rubra* and *scabrosa*, there is the additional bounty of bright berries, in size almost like young apples in the late autumn. Given sufficient space they make fine hedges.

Musk roses have been favourites in English gardens from the time of Queen Elizabeth I. One I particularly like is quite a modern one, a 1954 introduction, Magenta, which is on the borderline between a floribunda and a hybrid musk. About five feet tall, its double, richly scented flowers on large, branching sprays are lilac with reddish touches in the buds.

Of the modern shrub roses, Nevada is believed to be a hybrid of *R. moyesii*, but whatever its origin I look upon it as one of the finest additions to our gardens this century. It makes a bush about six or seven feet high with five-inch almost single flowers which begin creamy but open up to white, sometimes slightly tinged with pink, with rich golden stamens. Seen at the first flowering with the blooms almost touching over the bush, it is superb. Its rose-pink sport Marguerite Hilling is just as good.

Cabbage roses (*R. centifolia*) were once to be found in most cottage gardens and they also appear in many flower paintings, their full globular flowers nodding on gracefully curved stems. Except for the miniatures they grow into bushes about five or six feet high and flower in June and July with a rich scent. The Old Cabbage Rose itself dates back to the sixteenth century and has large, rose-pink cupped flowers and a scent best described as 'fruity'.

The moss rose (*Rosa centifolia muscosa*) is a sport from the cabbage rose and did not make its appearance until the eighteenth century. I like the Old Pink Moss, probably the oldest of them all, with its large, cup-shaped, beautifully scented rose-pink flowers, its fully mossed bush going up to around six feet.

Caroline Testout is a rose that tends to bring on a mild attack of nostalgia in me for when I began as a lad at Horwood House my way to work led through an archway where this rose grew in profusion and its perfume in summer was almost overpowering. A robust grower with rose-pink flowers it is one of the earliest hybrid teas and I still grow it both in climbing and bush form. Others that bring back pleasant memories are Betty Uprichard, General MacArthur (especially good in cold soils), Ophelia, Madame Butterfly and Frau Karl Druschki which had its name changed to Snow Queen in World War I.

146

It is amazing how many new roses have been introduced during my lifetime; yet only a comparative few have stood the test of time. Take Super Star, for example. I remember when Harry Wheatcroft exhibited this at the Chelsea Show, I think in 1959. Seeing it then with its blazing orange flame colour and dark healthy foliage I thought it almost perfect – possibly the rose of the century. Then that same August when I saw it at Shrewsbury Flower Show, outdoor-grown instead of from under glass as the Chelsea blooms had been, I was terribly disappointed. And it has gone from bad to worse; recently it has become increasingly prone to mildew.

Many people ask me about the Percy Thrower hybrid tea rose that is named after me. Naturally I am proud of this rose for I chose it myself. It was raised by Kordes in Germany and the stock of it bought by Gregory's of Nottingham who had it, together with several other new varieties, in their nursery. They asked me to choose one of these to be named after me. I went over to Nottingham and liked this particular rose but being a cautious man (gardening has taught me that) I requested it be given a longer trial before I decided if I wanted my name to be given to it. Gregory's kept it another two years in the nursery and when I saw it after this period, I liked it even more. The rose colouring was pleasant, the flower shape good, it lasted well in bud and also as a cut flower and was comparatively free from mildew and black spot. So I was glad to give my name to it, and now after eighteen years I still think it is a good rose and it has certainly proved a popular seller at my garden centre. Its only fault, perhaps, is that it is rather untidy in growth; it forms rather a lot of horizontal stems though this is more a worry to us when we have to pack it for despatch than for the customer. It has a delicate scent but not a strong one. It was introduced commercially in 1964 and Walter Gregory, the head of the Gregory rose firm at that time, asked if he could launch it at The Magnolias, which we did, putting up a large marquee and providing refreshments to accompany the bowls of Percy Thrower roses which were displayed everywhere for the benefit of the large number of visitors.

In the last year or so I have learned quite a lot about

timing roses to get them ready for a show. In 1975 and 1976 we made a rose garden at Shrewsbury Flower Show with roses grown in pots. The first year we cut back four weeks before the show and found that only certain varieties made it in time. The following year we cut back a week earlier and still some of the varieties did not make it. Those at their best were Fragrant Cloud, Piccadilly and Wendy Cussons, all hybrid teas. But floribundas such as Elizabeth of Glamis, News, Plentiful, Iceberg, Paprika, Border Coral and several others were not ready and we had to resort to putting those varieties which were in flower at the front of our garden exhibit and the others at the back. Because of this we had to be content with the award of a Gold Medal instead of a Large Gold Medal.

When I was at Windsor orchid growing was almost a religion. One man only was allowed to touch them. This specialist orchid grower had a greenhouse on a north-facing wall for his cymbidiums and a house on a west-facing wall for his odontoglossums and calanthes. Orchids in my young days were always regarded as plants beyond the understanding of the ordinary everyday gardener. But things have changed considerably in recent years: much new knowledge has been acquired about these exotic plants and what was once considered to be a millionaire's hobby involving costly greenhouses, expensive plants and materials such as osmunda fibre, sphagnum moss, charcoal and dry cow manure has now come within the reach of the average keen gardener. New methods of raising, together with the discovery that they will grow quite well in bark and peat, are chiefly responsible for this. Cymbidiums are possibly the easiest of the orchids to cultivate followed by the paphiopedilums. Others which may be grown in an amateur's greenhouse are Coelogyne cristata, dendrobiums, cattleyas and odontoglossums.

Bulbs of one kind or other must have a place amongst everyone's favourites and of course they are among mine. They are certainly excellent for naturalizing. At The Magnolias I planted large areas of the field grass area with daffodils, scattering them and planting where they fell, to give a drift effect. There is a snag in that the

The launching of the 'Percy Thrower' rose at The Magnolias with (left to right) the author, Walter Gregory and Eric Robinson

grass must not be cut until the foliage of these bulbs has died down, which means waiting until about June before the lawns can be mown. The trumpet varieties of narcissus such as King Alfred, Magnificence and Golden Harvest always look a picture with their bright flowers nodding gracefully above the foliage and the bright green new grass. Numerous large-cupped and small-cupped varieties, the late-flowering Pheasant's Eye and other *poeticus* varieties are all well suited for naturalizing along with eranthis, *Fritillaria meleagris*, snowdrops, muscari, ornithogalum and scillas.

149

Miniature bulbs look their best, I think, in a rock garden. In mine I have the hoop petticoat daffodil, *Narcissus bulbocodium*, *N. pseudo-narcissus* (the Lent lily), *N. triandrus albus* (angels' tears) crocus species, dog's tooth violet, chionodoxa, muscari, *Iris reticulata* and *I. danfordiae* and these are increasing as the years go by. Between the shrubs in my border on the left of the drive are masses of daffodils – they grow so fast that I have already had to dig them up and sort them out, putting back the largest and growing on the remainder in a part of the vegetable garden until they reach flowering size.

For bulbs in pots I always start off with pre-cooled daffodils, Roman hyacinths and the narcissus Paper White to flower in time for Christmas: these I follow with prepared hyacinths, early single and double tulips and Yellow Cheerfulness narcissi. When I was at Horwood House Father used the large urns in front of the house for bulbs. He planted a layer of King Alfred daffodils in the bottom of each urn covered them with compost and planted another layer on top. The result was always a wonderful display of daffodils all of the same height and flowering together. I adapted this for television and it was one of the most popular things I ever did. I took an eight-inch pot, put six Golden Harvest daffodil bulbs on the bottom, covered them with fibre and then put another eight bulbs of the same variety on top and covered these. It produced an absolute mass of flowers – more than forty blooms. And I had many letters from viewers saying how successful they, too, had been with this. I have also used King Alfred and Magnificence daffodils successfully for this, yet for some reason or other which I have not yet worked out the method does not seem to work with either hyacinths or tulips.

As for plants in general I find, like most other gardeners I expect, that my garden, fairly large though it may be, is just not big enough for all the different things I want to grow and for the many plants given to me by friends. There is more friendliness, I'm sure, among gardeners than in any other profession or occupation: gardeners are always wanting to help; ever anxious to provide another gardener with something he may not have

Daffodils always look well when naturalized in grass under trees

whether it be in the form of plant or knowledge. The result with me – for I visit more gardens than most I expect – is that I keep bringing things back and now it is a struggle to find places to put them.

I also think that most gardeners often aim at the impossible. I know I do. We are so determined to grow a plant we have perhaps seen and admired somewhere that we fail to realize that the location of our garden and other circumstances may be entirely unsuitable for it. I remember at Bodnant, where they have one of the finest collections of trees and shrubs anywhere in Britain, seeing *Embothrium coccineum* and *E.c. lanceolatum* (which I had only once seen before and that was at Castle Kennedy on holiday with my father) and being determined to grow them. Now embothrium is a rather tender evergreen shrub and only really suitable for a sheltered position which The Magnolias certainly does not enjoy. I planted both of these and I am glad to say that one of them, *lanceolatum*, is thriving – though I have to admit that at the time of writing it has not yet had to face a severe winter. When that happens it could be a different story. But at present it flowers freely and makes a marvellous display in the summer.

Another 'impossible' I've persevered with is *Eucryphia nymansensis*, an evergreen which seen in full flower in August is magnificent. In 1948 I was given a rooted cutting and grew it in the Dingle at Shrewsbury where it went up to fifteen feet. Every year in August it was a mass of flowers and everyone admired it. The cold winter of 1963, however, killed it stone dead. Yet I persevered. In 1964 I planted one at The Magnolias which has already gone up to ten feet and also flowers profusely every August. And every winter I say to myself, 'Will it survive?' – for I know in my heart that I ought not to grow this plant in our exposed conditions, but I do like it so.

On the other hand, in my experience every gardener has problem plants that present a challenge. One that I have had more trouble with than most is *Gentiana acaulis* which, in some positions in the garden, just won't move, let alone flower; replant it perhaps a few feet away and it suddenly starts spreading and flowering. I moved the

This technique of planting two layers of narcissus bulbs in one container became very popular as a result of a demonstration in a television programme

plant I had four or five times in the rock garden until this happened. The same with my plant of *G. sino-ornata*: I moved this at least three times before it would settle down and flower for me. One should never give up in gardening: that is one thing I have learnt over the years. A true gardener learns by his mistakes and is always willing to accept a challenge if a plant fails to do well with him; he will keep on trying until he succeeds. So for myself I would not say that there is anything I can't grow – but I have to admit that I am not 100 per cent. successful with quite a few things – but I keep on trying.

At The Magnolias I keep bedding plants down to a minimum. On the patio we have three tubs moulded in terracotta, four troughs and six smaller tubs. These, in late May and early June, are full of fuchsias, geraniums, trailing lobelias and petunias. The geraniums are the scarlet Paul Crampel and the red, variegated-leaved Caroline Schmidt; the fuchsias are Golindrina, Brutus, Mrs Marshall, Mrs Pearson, Cascade and Marinka. With regular watering and feeding (because the roots are restricted, the plants need more feeding than usual) these give a bright display from June until the first frosts of autumn. They are then replaced by daffodils, double and single early tulips, crocuses, wallflowers, forget-me-nots and sometimes polyanthus. As a result, when we walk out on to the terrace there is always something to look at and enjoy.

I don't go in for hardy annuals much these days except perhaps to raise a few for flower decorations and arrangements. Even dahlias, gladioli and chrysanthemums in the last year or two have had to give way more and more to vegetables. I like growing vegetables: I get a lot of pride and a sense of achievement in growing them well. Again I go back to my early days when the vegetable garden was kept as neat and tidy as any flower garden. Since the 'Dig for Victory' days of the last war we have seen a complete turn of the wheel. We have had a period when many gardeners could hardly be bothered with vegetables – why should they when they were so cheap in the shops? But now with the cost of vegetables soaring flower gardens and lawns are being turned over to vegetables. At The Magnolias I have a vegetable and fruit garden eighteen yards across at its widest point and forty yards long. That grows sufficient vegetables to keep us the year through with the exception of potatoes: I don't grow maincrop potatoes because up until now at least I have considered the ground could be put to more valuable use. But with the rising price of them in the shops I may have to change my mind. Apart from potatoes I have kept up a regular supply of fresh and good quality vegetables – this is absolutely essential for I am married to a head gardener's daughter who has always been used to the very best in this sphere. Anyway, there can be no doubt that home-grown produce, freshly gathered, has quite a different flavour to shop-bought produce. It is certainly cheaper.

In the greenhouse I like to grow melons, cucumbers, tomatoes, early strawberries and French beans to provide produce out of season. I also use cloches to obtain early salads, carrots and beetroot for pulling, onions and so on. Many new varieties of vegetables have put in an appearance in recent years but though I try out many of them I only continue if they really do have something better to offer. If one were to believe everything that is said and written about most new varieties one would think that they were all winners, which is far from being the case. Of course there are good ones, but I do not part with an old favourite until I am certain I have something better. So I tend to grow a mix of old and new varieties. Here are a few of them:

Beetroot: Crimson Globe, Sutton's Globe, Boltardy

Broad Beans: Imperial White Windsor, Aquadulce, Claudia, The Sutton (dwarf), Colossal, Masterpiece

Broccoli: Calabrese (Italian green sprouting), White and Purple Sprouting

Brussels Sprouts: Peer Gynt, Citadel (good freezers), Market Rearguard (late maturing)

Cabbages: (summer maturing) May Star, June Star, Hispi, Greyhound, Winnigstadt; (autumn) Market Topper, Autumn Supreme; (winter) January King; (spring) Offenham, Harbinger

Carrots: Amstel, Scarlet Horn, Chantenay Red Cored, Favourite, St Valery, Autumn King

Cauliflower: All the Year Round, Snowball, Snow's

A year-round supply of vegetables is essential when you are married to a head gardener's daughter

Winter White, St George, White Heart

Celeriac: Globus, Marble Ball, Alabaster

Celery: I still prefer the kind which needs earthing up such as Giant Red and Solid White. For self-blanching celery try Golden Self-blanching

Chicory: Witloof

Cucumbers: Improved Telegraph, Butcher's Disease Resister (good examples of old varieties that have stood the test of time), Femdan (a non-bitter, all female F_1 hybrid). For ridge cucumbers, Baton Vert

Endive: Exquisite Curled, Moss Curled, Batavian Green

French beans: The Prince (for early forcing), Masterpiece (maincrop), Canadian Wonder (late).

Kale: Pentland Brigg, Thousand-headed, Frosty

Kohl-rabi: Primavera White, Purple Vienna, White Vienna

Leeks: Musselburgh, The Lyon, Holborn Model

Lettuce: Cabbage type: All The Year Round, Continuity, Imperial Winter (for autumn sowing out of doors); May Queen, Tom Thumb (early Wonderful); Webb's

Cos Type: Little Gem (one of my real favourites, for it is very early, takes up little space and there is little waste), Winter Density

Melons: Dutch Net (orange-pink flesh, good for cultivation in a frame), Hero of Lockinge (white flesh and can be grown in either frame or greenhouse), Charantais, Superlative

Onions: Ailsa Craig, Autumn Queen, Bedfordshire Champion, Solidity

Parsnip: Tender and True, Hollow Crown

Peas: Feltham First, Kelvedon Wonder, Little Marvel (early), Onward, Dwarf Defiance (maincrop)

Potatoes: Sharpe's Express (still my favourite of the early potatoes), Majestic, Pentland Crown, Pentland Dell (maincrop)

Radish: French Breakfast, Cherry Belle, Black Spanish Round

Runner Beans: Kelvedon Wonder (very early), Streamline, Twenty-one (good for freezing), Scarlet Emperor, White Achievement, Hammond's Dwarf Scarlet, Hammond's Dwarf White (these last two are self supporting and need no staking)

Spinach: (summer) Long-standing Round, (winter) Broad-leaved Prickly, Long-standing Prickly

Swede: Purple Top, Bronze Top, Chignecto

Sweet Corn: First of All, Golden Bantam, John Innes Hybrid

Tomatoes: Alicante, Ailsa Craig, Moneymaker; The Amateur and Golden Amateur (bush), Outdoor Girl (for outdoor cultivation only)

Vegetable Marrows: Long Green, Long White, Table Dainty (trailing), Zucchini F_1 (courgette), Green Bush Improved, Tender and True (bush)

Fruit, like vegetables, is always best when eaten fresh from the garden. Every garden should have its fruit section for even where top fruits such as apples, pears, plums and cherries cannot be grown in tree form, because of lack of space, room can usually be found for such soft fruits as raspberries, gooseberries and currants while a few blackberries, loganberries and other hybrid berries can often be found a place in the corner of the garden or be trained on poles or fences. In many gardens, too, there are walls and fences where trained peaches and nectarines, pears, plums or sour cherries trained as fans may be grown. Another space-saving tip is to train apples and pears in cordon or espalier form as a hedge.

At The Magnolias I planted bush specimens of apples, pears and plums and cordon trees to screen the top of the vegetable garden. I installed a fruit cage for raspberries, blackcurrants and gooseberries but here I learnt a lesson. I covered the whole cage with wire netting and after three or four years I noticed that the raspberries were deteriorating, in fact they were dying away fast. I couldn't work out what was wrong but one day Arthur Billitt was here and he at once diagnosed the trouble as zinc oxide poisoning, the zinc oxide coming from the coating of the wire netting. I left the cage up, however, and I suppose the zinc oxide gradually wore off for the raspberries have improved considerably in recent years.

The raspberry is my favourite soft fruit, not only because it is so good to eat but because it produces fruit from June until late July, a time when it is really appreciated. Next comes the blackcurrant which also fruits well and is comparatively easy to grow. After that I would go for strawberries and gooseberries in that order. Strawberries are not a permanent crop, of course; three years is about the maximum for a bed and many gardeners even like to grow them as an annual crop. Gooseberries do not take up much room nor do they need a great deal of attention. As to varieties of these, for raspberries I like Malling Promise, Glen Clova, Malling Jewel, Norfolk Giant, Zeva and September. Blackcurrant varieties haven't changed much in recent years though Mendip Cross which comes nice and early is comparatively new and can be recommended while three good oldies are Wellington XXX, Boskoop Giant and Baldwin. Few of the strawberry names I knew as a boy are still with us for most have deteriorated too much to be worth growing now. Royal Sovereign which was once almost a household word retains its wonderful flavour but its cropping abilities are well below some of the more modern varieties and it is prone to virus infection. Other reliable varieties are Cambridge Vigour, Tamella, Cambridge Favourite and Redgauntlet which is a good mid-season variety. Hummi Grandi, with its exceptionally large berries of good flavour, has become popular. For an alpine strawberry I like Baron Solemacher, for perpetual-fruiting Sans Rivale and Gento. Gooseberries used to offer a choice of literally hundreds of varieties and gooseberry shows were a regular feature around Lancashire at one time. There are both dessert and culinary varieties and some which serve as both. They include Careless (culinary), Keepsake (dessert or culinary), Golden Drop (dessert, very suitable for the small garden), Lancashire Lad (a good jam maker), Leveller, Lancer and Whinham's Industry (all three dual purpose).

Apples offer a wide selection and the aim should be to have them in season over as wide a period as possible. To this end I suggest the following: Scarlet Pimpernel, dessert (August); Grenadier, culinary (August–October); James Grieve, dessert (September–October); Egremont Russet, dessert (October–December); Bramley's Seedling, culinary (November–March) – but the tree grows too large for small gardens; Cox's Orange Pippin, dessert (November–January); Lane's Prince Albert, culinary (November–February); Rosemary Russet, dessert (December–March); Winston, dessert (January–April). A household with these to choose from should never be short of apples up until May at least.

Pears, too, should be planted to provide a selection of fresh fruit over as long a period as possible. For dessert pears I suggest (in order of ripening) Doyenné d'Été (August); William's Bon Chrétien (September) – if this is picked a few days before ripe it will keep in a cool store for quite a while; Dr Jules Guyot (early September); Louis Bonne of Jersey (October); Beurré Hardy (October); Conference (October–November) needs to be picked and kept a few days before eating; Doyenné du Comice (November) my favourite of all pears though it can be a shy cropper; Packham's Triumph (November–December), a good bottler; Joséphine de Malines (December–January), keep this one for eating at Christmas. Two good cooking varieties are Bellissime d'Hiver which keeps from December until March and Catillac which is in season from December right up until April.

Plums, too, should be chosen to give a succession;

if only one tree is grown a variety that is self fertile should be obtained or it may not set fruit. I suggest the following if a really good succession of fruit is required. Rivers' Early Prolific, culinary (late July), though only partially self fertile it is very suitable for s.nall gardens and makes excellent jam; Early Laxton, dessert, partially self fertile (late July); Czar, culinary, self fertile (early August); Early Transparent Gage, dessert, self fertile (mid August); Victoria, dessert and culinary, self fertile (mid to late August); Pershore or Yellow Egg, culinary, self fertile (late August), a good jam maker as well as a cooker; Monarch, culinary, self fertile (end of September).

Cherries may be either of the sweet kind for eating or the sour kind for cooking. Sweet varieties in order of ripening I would recommend are: Early Rivers, Bigarreau de Schrecken, Elton Heart and Bigarreau Napoleon. For sour, Kentish Red and Morello.

For the lesser grown fruits may I suggest:

Apricots: Moorpark

Blackberries: Bedford Giant, John Innes, Merton Thornless

Loganberries: Thornless, especially the LY59 strain

Red currants: Laxton's No. 1, Red Lake

White currants: White Versailles, White Dutch

Figs: Brown Turkey

Grape Vines: (Under glass) Black Hamburgh, Madresfield Court, Muscat of Alexandria. (Outdoors on a warm wall) Buckland Sweetwater

Peaches: Hale's Early, Peregrine

Nectarines: Early Rivers

I could go on like this for page after page telling of other favourite plants of mine cultivated over a lifetime of gardening. I could speak of other likes and dislikes and provide many a hint and tip. But this is not really the time or place: most of these things will be found somewhere or other in my books on gardening. The more important thing to remember is that just as a garden gives according to what is put in it so you will get from your gardening in the way of pleasure and satisfaction what you care to put into it. Whatever you do, do it well, and you will have few regrets.

Pleasures and Rewards

My father once took me to Shrewsbury Flower Show when I was a boy and during my time at Windsor we young gardeners were allowed to go to the Chelsea Flower Show in London. But not until war came did I have much to do with horticultural shows and this arose through being asked to judge – mainly vegetables of course – during the 'Dig for Victory' days in and around the town of Derby.

For those who may be called upon to judge at a show let me at once recommend a little publication of the Royal Horticultural Society. This is *The Show Handbook – A Guide for Judges and Exhibitors* which is still available and invaluable to anyone having to judge at a show however large or small. And, of course, as its name implies, it is just as useful to an exhibitor, for it points out what the judges will be looking for when preparing their assessments.

After taking over as parks superintendent at Shrewsbury I began to be invited to judge at shows in the county of Shropshire and, gradually, as I became better known, further afield and at more important events. Quite early on I judged at the Derby Chrysanthemum Show, the Shrewsbury Chrysanthemum Society Show and at Cheltenham and Leamington Spa. Then came a step up, an invitation to judge the flower section of the Royal Show. And after that I went all over the place: Southport, City of Birmingham, Royal Highland, British Timken, City of Liverpool, Leicester, City of Manchester, Royal Cornish, Eastern Counties, Suffolk – these are some of the shows at which I have officiated.

Of all the shows in the country Chelsea ranks foremost: to most gardeners it is *the* show of the year. The first time I went as a young gardener I remember how astonished

I was at the superb displays – and I have remained astonished every time I have been since; which is a good many times for I have hardly missed a single one, though of course they were not held during the years of World War II. Over the years I have seen many changes yet I cannot honestly say that it is better now than when I first saw it back in the 1930s. Granted there is more variety and the scientific section is a good innovation which has much to teach gardeners, but I do miss the massive exhibits that Suttons, Carters and one or two others used to put on regularly.

Chelseas Show is, and as far back as I can remember, always has been, the subject of much heart searching on behalf of its members and of outside horticultural interests. The hierarchy of the Royal Horticultural Society is conservative in its attitude to change or innovation and this does not always go down well with the more progressive elements. The Society takes a lot of shifting from any position even if it is over something that may appear to others to be quite petty. One such is the rule that animals must not be introduced on any exhibit. An example of the silliness of this rule occurred

Judging a stand of dahlias at the British Timken Show. Godfrey Baseley, of the BBC, is second from the right

PLEASE DO

a few years ago when two of the largest garden supply firms in the country put on magnificent displays but had the 'audacity' to put live goldfish in their ornamental pools. They were at once ordered by the R.H.S. either to remove the goldfish or remove their exhibits! Almost the same thing happened with Murrells of Shrewsbury. Miss Murrell had designed a lovely garden of miniature roses which included a small pool in the centre for water lilies. As such a pool would not look right without a few fish Miss Murrell put in three goldfish. But the eagle eye of an R.H.S. official spotted them and out they had to go! And the fuss that was made in the garden sundries section at one time when the only items allowed to be sold for cash were gardening books and magazines.

As a result of all this, plus the fact that the costs of exhibiting are rising every year, many of the older exhibitors have left Chelsea while many potential newcomers have not taken space. More selling is now being allowed, I'm glad to say, and this could help alleviate the Society's financial position. But membership needs to increase considerably and I feel it will need a changed outlook on the part of some of those in authority if this is to be achieved and the Society put back on a sound footing.

Apart from Chelsea, Britain has a marvellous heritage of other shows throughout the land, particularly in the north of England where the industrial workers have always tended to keep the standard high. At Sheffield, for example, the miners raise some of the finest large exhibition chrysanthemums to be found anywhere while the standard at Derby Chrysanthemum Show is just as high. A great deal of time and experience goes into preparing these chrysanthemums in order to get the blooms at their peak for the day of the particular show.

Though I have taken part in hundreds, perhaps thousands, of shows either as exhibitor or judge, in only one have I been put on exhibition myself. That was, and is, at Madame Tussauds in London.

When I was around twelve or thirteen my elder brother took me to Madame Tussauds in Baker Street and I was fascinated by the wax models particularly those in the chamber of horrors which are almost frighteningly

lifelike in the dim and eerie lighting of the chamber.

How strange then one day to receive a telephone call, followed by a letter, from Madame Tussauds informing me that they were making a conservatory into which they wanted to place the figure of Percy Thrower in his capacity as 'the nation's head gardener'. Could they come to Shrewsbury and take measurements to make a wax model of me? It would be quite painless and not take up too much of my time. They also assured me that the model was definitely *not* intended for the chamber of horrors, not then or at any other time! Two girls arrived at The Magnolias; one had a camera with which she proceeded to photograph me from every angle imaginable while the other took my measurements very thoroughly. They had also brought samples of hair and eyebrows and these they checked with mine. Also a

A signing session at Chelsea Flower Show

rather gruesome-looking box of glass eyes from which they chose two that exactly matched mine in size and colour.

I heard later that the waxwork model had been completed and that I could go and see it anytime I chose. I never seemed to find myself in the Baker Street area, however, but one day I turned up at the BBC studios for a *Blue Peter* programme and I was told that a small surprise was in store for me. A little apprehensively I walked into the *Blue Peter* garden to be confronted with a most life-like model of myself, complete with muddy shoes, pipe and watering can. It was the Tussauds' waxwork model which they had borrowed. John Noakes, who was opening the programme, began by saying to the model, 'Hello, Percy, what do you think of the garden then?' Getting no answer he went on, 'Eh? It's not so bad as all that is it? I think he's speechless!' I then walked up and said, 'He might be . . . but I'm not,' and went and stood beside the model. Some time afterwards I did get along to Baker Street and see it in its proper surroundings – and I was happy to find that it really was in a conservatory – not in the chamber of horrors.

I am always happy to do what I can for charity, especially for any connected in some way with gardening. As I mentioned in the chapter on The Magnolias we open the gardens every year for charity. I have also made appeals on radio and television; one I did on television in 1976 in aid of the Royal Midland Counties Home for the Disabled at Leamington Spa brought in over £13,000: the appeal was connected with gardening inasmuch that many of the severely disabled at this home do gardening as part of their occupational therapy.

Although I have criticized the Royal Horticultural Society in connection with their annual show at Chelsea I have a great respect for the Society as an institution. As far as I know nothing else quite like it exists in the world. So when I was made an Associate of Honour of the Society I certainly did regard it as an honour. And when, in 1974, I was awarded the coveted Victoria Medal of Honour I was very moved indeed. To go to the Royal Horticultural Society's headquarters in London and be presented with it in the presence of many famous horticulturists was a touching occasion. As I sat in the hall waiting for my name to be called my mind went back over my career, to Horwood House and my father and a six-shillings-a-week wage; to Windsor and my friends of the bothy; to Leeds, Derby and Shrewsbury; and I felt proud yet humble to think that I had achieved what only a few of the famous old gardeners of my youth had achieved even at the end of a long career. But I could not help thinking that many had been overlooked; for example, my father-in-law C. H. Cook, head gardener at Windsor, and his brother Tom Cook, head gardener at Sandringham, who were among the foremost horticulturists in the land and who, in addition, had devoted a great deal of their time to the raising of money for gardening charities had never received any recognition from the R.H.S. for their efforts.

If the Victoria Medal of Honour is the highest award horticulture can offer to its gardening sons, to appear on *This is Your Life* must be one of the highest honours the medium of television offers anyone who has been in the public eye. It is a recognition, I suppose, that one is known to many people and that they will be interested to know more about one's life and background.

Many a time I had watched Eamonn Andrews and his *This is Your Life* programme never dreaming that the day would come when I would be the subject of one. When it did come – in March 1976 – I can truthfully say that I was taken completely by surprise. Watching the programmes I had always felt that the 'victim' *must* know something about what was going on: it was such an elaborate set-up and involved so many people and needed such careful timing that I was convinced that some collaboration had taken place. Yet this had always been denied by the participants.

So how did they set me up? First of all let me say that it came out later that my wife and family had known about it and were working on it for six months before the day. Yes, six months, and I had not the faintest idea that anything out of the ordinary was going on. I even walked into the house one night much earlier than expected and finding the kitchen table covered with all the old family photographs said to Connie, 'What's all this about?' and accepted without the slightest suspicion her explanation that she was just going through them to sort them out.

Then I was to go up to London to attend Flora 76 and Peter Wood, editor of *Amateur Gardening*, (the magazine was one of the sponsors of Flora 76) phoned to say that he had a new photographer and was anxious to have a picture of me in the gardens of the Ideal Homes Exhibition at Olympia which was on at the same time as Flora 76. This phone call came some two months before the event which I suppose should have made me a little suspicious but being used to the strange ways of the Press I accepted without a further thought. Anyway, it was quite normal to be asked to be photographed by some paper or other.

Flora 76 came and I gave the opening talk in the morning. I was being watched, I learnt later, to see that I did not do anything out of character such as suddenly disappearing or forgetting I had an appointment later with the photographer. Peter Wood arrived and took me out to lunch at the 'Old Cheshire Cheese' in Fleet Street which was very pleasant and put me in a cheerful mood. That over I went to my hotel for a short rest, Peter having said that he would pick me up at tea-time and take me to Olympia where we were due at five o'clock for the photographing.

At the Ideal Homes Exhibition one of the first things I saw on entering was a television camera with a light on and a microphone over the top. The gardens were also lit up for television. This was all a familiar sight to me and I remarked, 'They're doing television from here?' to which Peter, without turning a hair, replied, 'They're always doing television at the Ideal Homes Exhibition.' Quite unsuspicious still, I walked on and passing some plastic cherry trees jokingly pointed them out and remarked, '*Prunus plasticiensis*, no doubt?' Peter laughed ˙ and then the photographer arrived and began to pose me by a bay tree and, handing me a pair of secateurs, took a picture of me pruning. Then he led me to a bed of tulips and asked me to pretend to be doing something with one of the plants. All this time I could still see the television cameras and why I was so dumb I can't think. Anyway I reached over to the tulips and as I did so there

166

came a burst of laughter and I thought someone must have fallen in the water or something. At the same moment I felt a tap on my shoulder and a voice I had heard before saying: 'Excuse me, I just want to interrupt these photographs for a second . . . .' I looked up and it was Eamonn Andrews holding a book and a microphone. I said enquiringly, 'Hallo?' and then he went on '. . . because, Britain's head gardener of radio and television fame, Percy Thrower, tonight – This is Your Life!'

Even then I didn't quite grasp it: it all struck me as funny for some reason or other and I began to laugh and said something like, 'This is a joke, isn't it?' but Eamonn said, 'You've planted a few surprises in your time, Percy, now here's one for you.'

I went off with Eamonn and his staff in a kind of daze.

'This is a joke, isn't it?'

When we arrived at the studio a crowd of teenagers were screaming their heads off and I wondered if they had anything to do with me – but I needn't have worried; they were waiting for some pop star.

I was put in a dressing room where on a table was gin, tonic water, champagne and cigars. 'Sit down and make yourself comfortable,' they said, but they never left me – not for a moment. I noticed a shirt and tie on a hanger in a corner and asked why they had put me in someone else's dressing room. 'Oh, no,' they said, 'the shirt and tie are yours – your wife brought them in because she knew that the shirt you went out in this morning was not suitable for television.' And I had to change. A little later I was taken along a corridor, escorted all the way and not allowed to deviate to right or left in case I met someone I was not supposed to see, and arrived in the studio where Eamonn and all his technical staff were waiting.

Things began to happen so quickly that I just didn't have time to get worried or frightened. Eamonn began by saying that as a tribute to the 'gardener's lad who was to become the nation's head gardener with literally millions following his advice in newspapers, radio and television', would I watch the screen in front of me on which I would see and hear from just a few of my 'devoted followers'.

On to the screen came Isobel, Lady Barnett, in her garden at Leicester, and she spoke of the days when we had worked together on afternoon television and how I had given her many gardening hints and how she had picked my brains. She finished by saying, 'Anytime you're passing, do pop in because . . . I'm having a little trouble with a cypripedium orchid . . .'

Isobel was followed by actor Simon Williams, The Hon. James Bellamy of the television series *Upstairs, Downstairs*. Speaking from his conservatory he said that he had once called me the 'Dr Spock of the garden world' but that I had replied that *I* had never had to get up in the middle of the night to attend a rose bush with colic.

Next on the screen appeared singing star Vince Hill who, speaking from his greenhouse, said: 'Do you remember this place . . . the very same you came to for a look at my cucumbers?' He went on: 'I well remember when we knew you were coming my wife Ann and I came out into this greenhouse, gave it a good clean up and made it look spick and span. And I'll never forget your first words when you came in here. You took one look around and said, "That's what I like to see . . . just like mine. A real scruffy greenhouse". However, you did cure my cucumbers and they went from strength to strength . . . just like yourself.'

(I had been to see Vince's cucumbers – and his tomatoes as well – because the fruits of both had developed some very peculiar shapes. I was able to identify the cause as damage from selective weed killer. And another thing, though Vince probably never knew it, I was nearly a guest on his own *This is Your Life* which went out shortly before mine. I had agreed to take part but about

A red leather volume containing photographs of the programme is presented to each 'victim' of *This Is Your Life*

two weeks before the programme was to go on I was rung up and told that they were very sorry but now that they had studied the script there would not be time to fit me in. I found out later that this was not the real reason: it was that my *This is Your Life* was to follow closely after Vince's and it would have looked slightly odd to see me in both of these programmes.)

Then the screen showed the *Blue Peter* programme and the legpull with the waxwork model of myself that I have described earlier on in this chapter. The picture faded from the screen and through the door of the studio came Lesley Judd of *Blue Peter*. She said that I had always managed to explain the complications of gardening in terms that she and her colleagues John Noakes and Peter Purves were able to understand but that one member of the team took whatever I said rather too literally — he never stopped digging. It was, of course, Shep the dog who had dug up many a seedling I had planted in the *Blue Peter* garden. And in came Shep with Peter Purves who informed me that Shep was not only asking my forgiveness for digging up the seedlings but also for regarding all Percy Thrower plants that stood upright as lamp posts.

Then Eamonn dwelt on my years as a 'royal gardener' and announced to the audience that I had made a name for myself almost as soon as I arrived at Windsor. I wondered what was coming and then a voice that I didn't recall but knew I had heard before said, 'That was because Percy started by courting the head gardener's daughter'. It was no wonder I found the voice a little difficult to place for I had not heard it for over forty years: it belonged to one of the lads who had been in the bothy with me at Windsor, Bob Musk. Seeing him in the flesh again brought back many memories. Bob went on to enlarge about me courting the head gardener's daughter. 'Lads of the bothy,' he said, 'were not even allowed to look at the head gardener's daughters . . . but when we found that Percy had the nerve to start courting Connie we realized that he was destined for something greater.'

Then, on cue, in came my wife Connie and my three daughters Margaret, Susan and Ann. Then Connie's sister Mabel was mentioned and the viewers were told how

A family group taken at Susan's twenty-first birthday party. Left to right: Ann, Margaret, Father, Mother and Susan

she had been in on all the secrets of our courtship. 'And where's Mabel now?' Eamonn asked, all innocent-like. 'In Newfoundland', Connie told him, 'she's been living there these last thirty years.' I didn't realize what it was leading up to until Eamonn announced, 'But the girl who helped to bring you two together . . . is not in Newfoundland, Canada. Tonight we have flown her three thousand miles to join you again and here she is!' And through the doorway came Mabel . . . it was just unbelievable!

My brothers and sisters followed, then Ken Hodgkinson whom I have spoken of in my chapter on Derby Parks, Arthur Billitt (who had been with me that morning and had excused himself saying that he had a meeting in the afternoon!) and then, totally unexpected, someone I had never met but whom I remembered writing to with

regard to some query or other. It was none other than the famous film actress, writer and director, Mai Zetterling. ITV had flown her all the way from Sweden to take part in the programme. In her delightful accent she said: 'I was a fan, a very great fan of yours, Percy. My husband knew about it and wrote asking if you would be kind enough to send me a letter for Christmas . . . with some advice about growing lilies. And,' she went on, 'do you know what I think you did. I think you sent your greenfingers in that letter. Because those lilies, because of what you said, grew into the most *indecent* lilies . . . not five, or ten, blooms . . . there were fifteen, twenty, twenty-five . . . quite frightening!'

The next surprise was the appearance of the daughter of Herr Witte, the parks superintendent of Berlin with whom I had built the English Garden in that city back in 1951.

Harry Wheatcroft, a friend whom I had known personally since the war years and of for many years before that came bounding in carrying a large bunch of the Percy Thrower rose. I regard Harry as one of the greatest characters and publicity agents that British horticulture has ever had. He was outstanding wherever he put in an appearance. A great rose grower, he has probably promoted the rose industry more than anyone else in modern times. He used to pull my leg when we met and I pulled his. On this occasion he spoke about the rose that had been named after me. 'I've had him in a bed at home for many years,' he said, 'he's rather a spreading grower, so to keep him in I planted Madame Butterfly all around him . . . and he has behaved very well ever since.'

He went on to say that he had known me for over thirty years and kindly said that I had done more than any person he knew to help Britain become even more beautiful than ever. 'He is virile, active, he hasn't got the middle age spread the same as me: a true gardener and

Among the guests on *This Is Your Life* was Ursula Stoye, the daughter of the late head gardener of the English Garden in Berlin

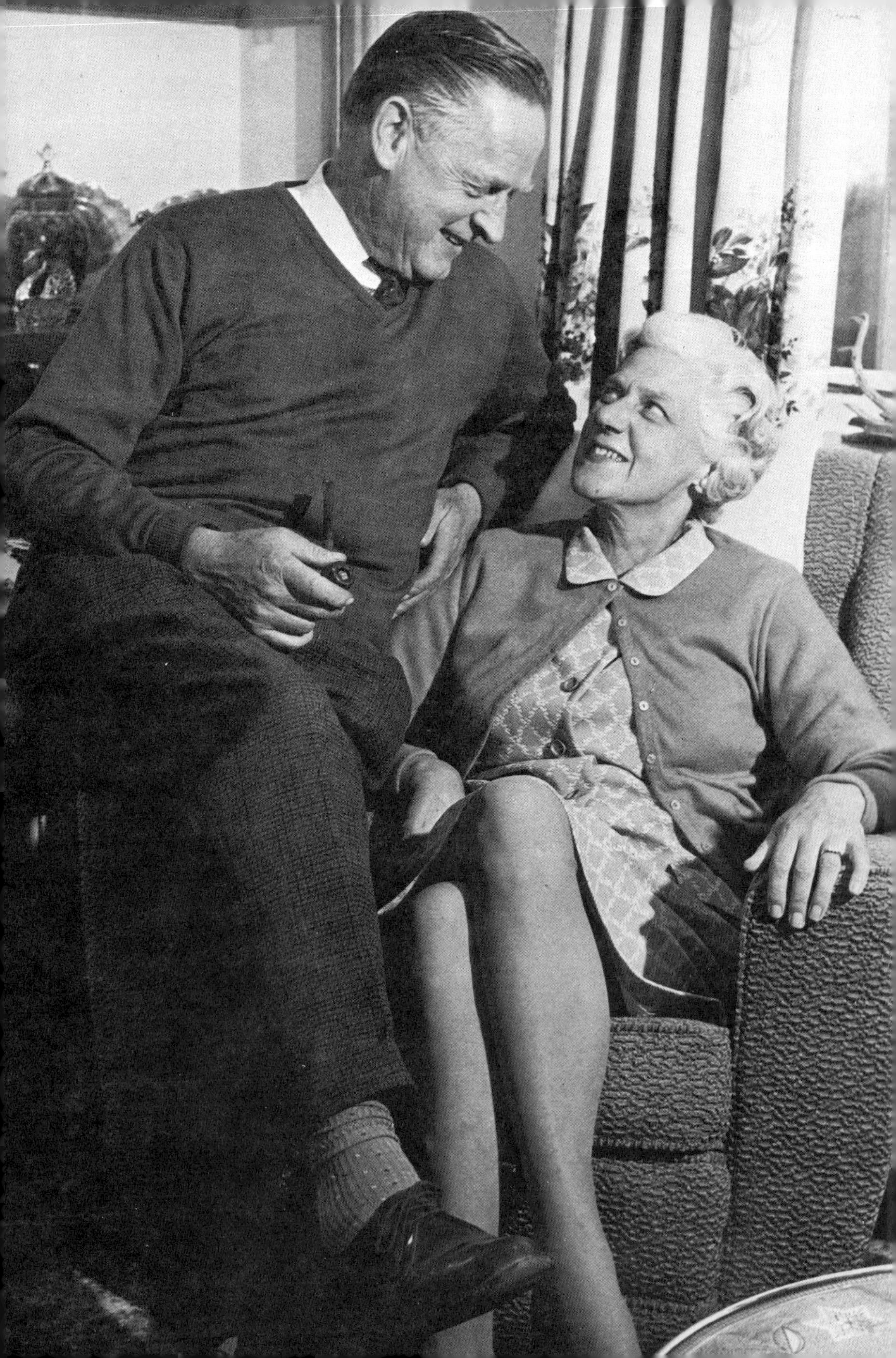

I am sure every gardener in England is toasting him tonight.' Harry's words moved me considerably.

The official part of the *This is Your Life* ended with a reunion of bothy boys from Windsor most of whom I had not seen for over forty years. But the unofficial celebrations went on late into the night and when it was all over I knew I had been through one of the most moving experiences of my life. Even now, when I look through the album of photographs that I was presented with or listen to the record of the proceedings, the memories come crowding back and I think to myself how lucky I am to be blessed with such a family and friends and to be able to have lived such a full life in the world of gardening.

I realize my life has been fulfilled in almost every way I can think of or wish for. I began my story by saying that from my earliest days I wanted to be a gardener and that my one ambition was to be a head gardener like my father. Well, I have been a gardener all my life and in recent years I have had the honour of being called Britain's Head Gardener. Thus I think I have fulfilled my ambition to an extent few can hope for. What can any man want more?

At home with Connie

Acknowledgements

The author and publishers would like to thank the following
for the illustrations used in this book:

Amateur Gardening 110, 111, 112, 113, 114, 140, 142, 145, 155, 163
BBC Copyright 89, 91, 95, 97
BBC Television *Blue Peter* 120
Country Life 8, 9, 18, 19, 30
Daily Express 149
Derby Corporation Parks Department 67, 69
Derbyshire County Library 59, 60
Graeme of Twickenham 128, 131
Humex Ltd. 115
IPC Magazines Ltd. 123
Carl & Pat Jameson 94
Jon Lyons 126, 135, 174
John Rea Studios 170
Shropshire Horticultural Society 44, 76
Thames Television 167, 172
West Midland Photo Services 85
J. E. J. Whitaker 82, 83
K. A. Wilding 41, 116